"The timing of our reading this book could not have been more perfect. When we went to see preschools for Brad we really felt prepared. It was great because all of the things in the book really applied in the situation—we knew exactly what was going on."

Joanne Kesler
Hillsborough, NC
Mother of a severely handicapped preschooler

"I think it is a terrific book! Very pertinent, organized, and readable."

Terriann Chubb
Chapel Hill, NC
Mother of a handicapped preschooler

"The book lets you know that other people are going through the same type of things that you are—and you can really profit from others' experiences."

Anne Lever
Chapel Hill, NC
Mother of 5-year-old with cerebral palsy

"This comprehensive and supportive guide will be extremely useful to parents as they try to find or structure an educational program for their handicapped preschooler. Frequently, parents find it difficult to reconcile their desire to do everything possible for their afflicted child and their duty to meet the legitimate needs of other family members. The authors' emphasis on the well-being of the entire family and on realistic expectations for the preschooler and his education should help alleviate the resulting parental guilt. As the mother of a young multiply-handicapped child, I highly recommend this book."

Helen Harrison
Berkeley, CA
Author of The Premature Baby Book

"This book is a boon to professionals working with young children and their families. It helps put the child's needs in the proper context of the needs of the parents and of the family as a whole. Having a view from the parents' perspective, professionals can be better prepared to meet parents halfway on issues such as program selection, preparation of children (and parents) for preschool, developing the IEP, and home training programs.

Janet Wedel
Lawrence, KS
Director, Kansas Early Education Program

SELECTING A PRESCHOOL

A GUIDE FOR PARENTS OF HANDICAPPED CHILDREN

Pamela J. Winton, Ph.D.
Formerly, University of North Carolina at Chapel Hill

Ann P. Turnbull, Ed.D.
University of Kansas, Lawrence

Jan Blacher, Ph.D.
University of California, Riverside

University Park Press
Baltimore

UNIVERSITY PARK PRESS
International Publishers in Medicine and Human Services
300 North Charles Street
Baltimore, Maryland 21201

Typeset by The TypeWorks
Manufactured in the United States of America by The Maple Press Company
Designed by Barry Goldman Designs, Baltimore

Library of Congress Cataloging in Publication Data
Winton, Pam
  Selecting a preschool

  1. Handicapped children—Education (Preschool)—United States—
Handbooks, manuals, etc.   I. Turnbull, Ann P, 1947–
II. Blacher, Jan.   III. Title.
LC4019.2.W56   1983   371.9   83–7020
ISBN 0–8391–1890–2

Contents

Preface

This is an exciting and challenging time for parents of handi-capped children. New laws, such as P.L. 94–142, the Education for All Handicapped Children Act, and new practices, such as keeping handicapped children in home settings rather than placing them in institutions, have meant increased responsibili-ties for parents and more opportunities for children. Never be-fore have the rights of handicapped children to an appropriate education been so clearly stated. Yet research indicates that the translation of law into practice is far from easy. Services guaran-teed by law are not available in many communities. Parents who rather suddenly have been put into the position of making sure their handicapped children receive an appropriate education often do not have the information they need to function effec-tively in this role. For instance, mainstreaming is an important issue for parents to consider in deciding upon the most appro-priate education for their child; yet in a nationwide survey we recently conducted, 95% of the parents of young handi-capped children interviewed wanted more information about mainstreaming.

As professionals and as parents we started asking ourselves why the type of information that is vital to parents being able to function effectively in a decision-making role was not readily available for the parent audience. Research and policy analyses of decision-making issues are extensively covered in the profes-sional literature. We realized that, within the academic commu-nity, writing for professionals is the priority, rather than writing for consumer audiences. For the most part, research projects

Parts of Dr. Blacher's contributions to this book were prepared while she was on sabbatical at Harvard Medical School and at Judge Baker Guidance Center.

The preparation of this book was supported by the U.S. Dept. of Educa-tion, Office of Special Education, Contract Number 300–77–0309.

are funded for short periods of time—one to two years. Unless a project is geared directly toward the development of materials for parents, rarely is time and money left at the end of a research project to translate and synthesize the findings for a parent audience.

We have been fortunate in that the research we conducted with parents was a part of the Carolina Institute for Research in Early Education for the Handicapped, one of four early child-hood research institutes funded over a five-year period (1977–1982) by the United States Bureau of Education for the Handicapped in the Department of Education. (The name of this office has recently been changed to Special Education Programs.) This grant enabled us to proceed in a far different way than we would have if given only a time frame of one to two years within which to work. First of all, we were able to begin our series of research studies with intensive interviews with 31 parents. In doing this, parents defined for us the relevant issues associated with the preschool choice, rather than our defining the issues and giving them a narrow range of questions and answers from which to choose. After one of our interviews, a mother, seasoned by two years of participation in various re-search studies, made this comment:

I'm so glad someone's talking to me instead of
giving me forms to fill out and questionnaires. Last time
I said, "There are no answers to any of these questions."
They really should do some checking before they ask
some of these questions, because some of us don't even
know what you're talking about because of the language
the questions are stated in. I've got a handicapped
youngster—talk to me on my level.[1]

Secondly, we were able to take what we learned from our research studies and develop this book for parents. According to parents, some of the best sources of information and ideas are other parents of handicapped children. What we have tried to do in this book is to provide a framework in which the experi-

---

[1] Reprinted from Winton, P. J., and Turnbull, A.P. 1982. Dissemination of research to parent. *The Exceptional Parent*, 12(4):34.

ences of parents of handicapped children are interspersed with relevant information on research, laws, and policies.

Without the help, candor, and honesty of the original parents that we interviewed, the subsequent research and the book would not have been possible. The many quotes in the book come primarily from this group. We would like to thank Ceci Abrahamson, Lucy Brinkley, Sandra Brown, Barbara Byrd, Kylie Cranford, Peggy Ellison, Jean Hanchey, Brenda Harvin, Karla Hayes, Rita High, Deborah Hilton, Ann Johnson, Claudette Jones, Ruth Kearse, Charles and Arlena Lawrence, Ann Lever, Sally Markham, Johnnie McDougal, Grace Morgart, Norma Murphy, Trudy Payne, Mary "Phyllis" Pruitt, Portia Reese, Betty Reeves, Carolyn Register, Julia Ross, Kathy Sims, Jan Thomas, Melinda "Faye" Thompson, Caroline Tomlinson, Linda Walker, Sandy Ward, and Ann White.

A two-phased, field-testing approach was used in developing the book. We would like to thank Jim Hamilton, project officer, for his help in devising a field-test plan. Thanks to the following persons who reviewed an extensive outline of the book and made suggestions and comments during phase one of field testing: Marie Bristol, Dot Cansler, Judy Fromm, Pam George, Sue Goldstein, Kate Thegen, Pat Wesley and Mike Woodard. During phase two of our field testing, the following parents reviewed a draft of our manuscript, rated each chapter on a standardized questionnaire, and talked with one of the authors about revisions and changes: Suzanne Bair, Terriann Chubb, Susan Davis, Helen Harrison, Peggy Hibbert, Joanne and Russ Kesler, Kathi Korobka, Ann Lever, and Tony and Jean Mulvihill. From beginning to end, the writing of this book has depended upon the time and energies of a number of parents. It has been shaped by their perspectives from the initial research study to the final decisions about what to include in the book. To all of these parents: we thank you for the gift of your time, energy, honesty, and willingness to share.

Valuable editorial contributions were generously made by Bruce Baker, Virginia Huguley, and Janet Wedel. Research assistance for compiling the resources section was provided by Janice M. Allen, Cynthia Kahn, Karen McBride, and Kay Cech Wood. Manuscript preparation was provided by Thelma Dillon,

Jon Gaines, Mary Beth Johnston, Lori Llewellyn, and Jean Roberts of the Bureau of Child Research at the University of Kansas and by Betty Medved at the University of California, Riverside. David Lutz, the photographer, contributed his expertise, and Nancy Peterson and Lynda Schoonmaker provided assistance in obtaining both the photographs and the consents for them. We gratefully acknowledge their important contributions.

The book would not have been possible without the support of Dr. James Gallagher, Director of the Carolina Institute for Research in Early Education of the Handicapped. Dr. Gallagher's support of our desire to disseminate information directly to parents enabled us to undertake this project. Gratitude is also due to Dr. Richard Schiefelbusch, Director of the Bureau of Child Research at the University of Kansas, who provided time and resources to Ann Turnbull to complete her commitments to the Carolina Institute for Research in Early Education of the Handicapped after she moved from North Carolina to Kansas two years ago. We are indebted to both of these outstanding leaders for making this opportunity possible. In addition, the University of California, Riverside, generously made facilities and grant support available to Jan Blacher, which aided her in the completion of this effort.

Finally, we wish to acknowledge Janet S. Hankin and Susan Oliver at University Park Press. It has been a pleasure to work with them on the publication of this book.

Introduction

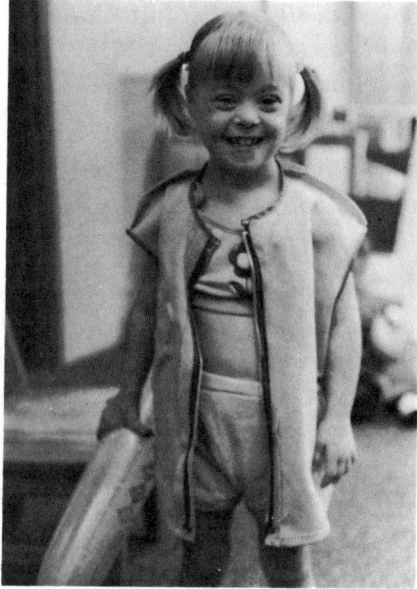

HOW
TO
USE THIS BOOK

"Where do we go from here? We have had this wonderful infant program to help us with our handicapped son's problems, but when he turns three he will no longer be eligible for these services. What's next? And how do we find it?"

"I am so confused. I know I can't relax the way I did with my older daughter because Susan's development and progress isn't something that happens naturally. I know it is crucial that I find her the best possible preschool education. But knowing that and finding a program are two different things. I am not even sure what I should be looking for. I feel like I have to figure out a system for approaching this task, but can't seem to get started."

*"What kind of preschool would be best for Jenny,
who has mild cerebral palsy? The physical therapist who
has worked with us since Jenny's infancy has told us
that Jenny would benefit now from being around more
children, and that we should look for a regular
preschool for her. But how do we find one? What if other
children make fun of her?"*

*"What about mainstreaming? Is that good or bad
for handicapped children? I hear so many conflicting
opinions. I would like to know what parents who have
tried it have to say about their experiences."*

*"I know that there are laws that give me and my
child certain rights, but how do those laws affect us at
the point where we are now? Do these laws mean I can
expect certain services at the preschool level? I have
heard about the IEP, but how does my child get one?"*

These are some comments made by a group of mothers whose
children were approaching "graduation" from an Infant Treatment Program at the University of North Carolina. Unfortunately, these feelings and frustrations are not limited to this one
group of parents and are not restricted to the Chapel Hill, N.C.,
area. One woman, who is the parent of a handicapped child,
sister of a handicapped adult, and a board member of the San
Francisco Bay Center for Educational Services, comments about
her own experiences and observations:

*I am aware of the tremendous struggles that families in
this sophisticated and liberal community have in
finding help for their impaired children. Often excellent
programs exist, but parents and professionals are
unaware of them. To a great extent this is because there
is a lack of coordinated services, a lack of publicity
about services that exist, and uncertain funding—a
program may be here today and gone tomorrow. I am
appalled by the lack of knowledge about programs that I
see among professionals who counsel parents. To take
our own example, even though our child was diagnosed
soon after birth as 1) cerebral palsied, 2) retarded, 3)*

*functionally blind, and 4) hydrocephalic, we were never
directed by the followup clinic staff, the pediatrician,*
numerous *psychologists, our ophthalmologist, or the
neurosurgeon to any program that could help us or our
son. Every school and preschool our son has attended
has been through a chance discovery on our part. He
currently attends a wonderful school in San Francisco
that I found through a woman I met in a cooking class.
Our experiences are not unique. During a meeting at my
son's preschool attended by close to 50 parents, almost
every set of parents expressed anger that they had found
out about the school through word of mouth,* not *from a
professional.*

HOW THIS BOOK CAME ABOUT

During the years 1977–1982, a series of research studies with
parents of young handicapped children was carried out by the
authors at the Frank Porter Graham Child Development Center,
University of North Carolina at Chapel Hill. One of these studies
involved in-depth interviews with 31 parents of young handicapped children. The focus of these interviews was on how
parents locate preschool programs, how they decide upon a
particular program, and what they like and dislike about their
child's and their own experiences in these programs. Two messages became clear as a result of this study. One message was
that finding appropriate preschools for young handicapped children can be a difficult, frustrating, and time-consuming task for
parents. In most communities there is no one person or place
where parents can find out about which programs are available
and which children are eligible for particular programs. The
second message was that families approach this task in an individual way. The idea of a source book to serve as a decision-
making guide for parents developed out of this research.

WHAT THIS BOOK TRIES TO DO

One parent of a three-year-old handicapped child describes the
preschool decision as an experience comparable to finding

oneself at a major intersection with roads leading in every direction, and having no roadmap. The confusion is understandable. New laws, federal and state, have been created that have completely changed what parents of handicapped children can expect from public education. Relatively new educational practices, such as educating handicapped children in regular classrooms with nonhandicapped children, are being implemented. These changes have generated a range of options for the preschool education of handicapped children. Too often, however, when it comes to actually locating the services and programs promised by law, parents find themselves feeling confused over the types of available programs and the specific program best suited to the needs of their child.

State laws regarding the education of preschool handicapped children are not the same from state to state, and how these laws are actually carried out varies tremendously from community to community. This means that the preschool choices in one community can be vastly different from the choices in another community. The method of implementing new approaches, such as mainstreaming, also differs from place to place. This may be the reason why mainstreaming is praised by some people and harshly criticized by others. As the parent of a young handicapped child, you may feel caught in the middle of complicated laws and conflicting opinions. Unfortunately, there is no simple formula or easy answer to the question, "How do I find and select the best possible preschool experience for my child?" However, there is information that can be extremely important in helping you through this process. The purpose of this book is to bring this information together in a way that will help you to develop your own roadmap for locating the best possible preschool choice for your child in your own community.

HOW TO USE THIS BOOK

This book is based on the assumption that each family has unique ways of making decisions and unique needs in terms of information helpful for reaching a decision. This assumption is reflected in the way the book is organized. Information from many sources and on many topics is provided within the chapters of each of the six sections. This information includes laws and policies affecting handicapped children, research on the outcomes of preschool educational programs, guidelines and suggestions for educational decision making, and anecdotal accounts from mothers and fathers of young handicapped children who have been through the decision-making process themselves. The information has been organized in such a way that you can read selectively. Some chapters or sections may have information you need now. Other sections may not be relevant for you but may be important at some later date.

Perhaps the best way to orient yourself to the book is to take a few minutes to look over the Table of Contents. Looking at the chapter titles, which are in the form of questions, will give you an idea about where information on various topics can be found.

Some of your questions may not have simple, straightforward answers. The information you need may be in several places in the book. As a further introduction to the book, additional questions about the preschool experience are posed on the next few pages. References are made to specific chapters in this book where more information on each question can be found. Looking over these questions may be of further help to you as you decide where you want to begin your reading.

1. **Question: Why should I consider a preschool program for my child?**

   This first question is basic to the entire decision-making process. You may wonder if it really is necessary to begin the relationship (and that's what it is) with the schools in your community so early in your child's life. Chapter 1 is the place to begin reading if you have this question. It contains reasons why programs and services for your young handicapped child can be extremely important. The perspective that it offers is that your best course of action is to seek some sort of outside help from the resources in your community, because this approach works well for most families. However, each family is unique. For various reasons this may not be the best approach for you. The information in this book may be something you want to keep in reserve until you feel it is the time for you and your child to become involved in the programs and services in your community.

2. **Question: How do I figure out what I want from a preschool program?**

When you think about it, you know more about your child and your family than anyone else does. For instance, you know what your child can and cannot do in daily situations, what you would like your child to do to make his (or her) or your own life easier, and what your family's needs are for support and help. You are the resident expert on your child and your family, and the information you possess is vitally important in the planning of an educational program for your child. This is a fact recognized by most professionals.

In spite of this, many parents feel stymied when trying to translate what they know about their child and family into the language of professionals. Chapters 2 and 3 focus on child and family needs—how to determine them, prioritize them, and translate them into language used by professionals.

3. **Question: Are there certain types of preschools that are best for handicapped children?**

There is no simple answer as to what type of preschool is "best"; however, much has been written on the subject which may be helpful as you think about your situation. Chapters 4 and 5 include information on how attitudes towards and education of handicapped children have changed over time. A particular focus in both chapters is the concept of mainstreaming. The point that is made in this section is that good, bad, or mediocre programs of all types can be found. Probably the best way to figure out what is "best" for your child is to go out in your community and look carefully at what goes on in the preschools that are available.

4. **Question: What qualities should I look for when I visit preschools?**

A basic premise to remember is to let your choice of a preschool be guided by your child's and family's needs. A preschool that is known for its success in fostering creativity and artistic expression may not be the best choice if your child's greatest need is to develop self-help skills. Chapter 8 includes specific questions for you to consider as you visit different preschools. Also provided is a Decision Checklist which will help you match what you need from a preschool with the characteristics of the preschools that are available.

5. **Question: Where do I start in locating a preschool program for my child?**

The first consideration is your state of residence. If your state law provides public preschool education for handicapped children, start by contacting the Director of Special Education in your local school system. (Table 6.2 in Chapter 6 contains information on which states guarantee a *free* and *appropriate* preschool education for handicapped children.) The Director of Special Education should inform you of the procedure by which you and representatives of the school systems *together* will reach a decision about the best programs for your child. The importance of your being familiar with this procedure and with your rights and responsibilities for involvement in it cannot be overemphasized. Chapters 6 and 7 are the sections for you to read if you want more information about the decision-making process in states guaranteeing public preschool education.

If the state in which you live does *not* guarantee public preschool education, there is no one place to start. Chapter 8 includes specific suggestions on how to find out about services and programs that exist in your community.

6. **Question: What if I am dissatisfied with what I find in my community?**

How to proceed if you are dissatisfied very much depends upon what you are dissatisfied with, how dissatisfied you are, your own particular style, and the amount of energy you are willing to invest in trying to make changes. Your level of satisfaction may depend somewhat on how successfully you are able to monitor your child's progress in the preschool; Chapter 11 contains a description of the monitoring process and provides strategies for you to use. If you are dissatisfied with the services provided in your community for preschool handicapped children, and the state law guarantees a free and appropriate education for preschoolers, then you have a legal right to demand services. A formal mechanism exists (due process hearings) for resolving disagreements between you and the educational system. Chapter 6 contains an outline of your rights and of due process procedures. Chapter 12 includes an outline of strategies to use to best ensure that you and your child get the type of program and the services you need.

7. **Question: Once I have selected a preschool, how do I prepare my child for this experience?**

   How and to what extent you wish to prepare your child for the preschool experience depends entirely on your own unique situation. If your child is entering a preschool with other children very much like him or her, and with a staff accustomed to teaching and caring for such children, then you may not feel the need to make a lot of special preparation for the new school. If your child is entering a preschool where the opposite is true, then you may want to consider spending more time preparing for this situation. Our research with parents of preschool handicapped children indicates that handicapped children and their parents may experience a difficult period of adjustment when they first begin a preschool program in which teachers are not used to having handicapped children. In Chapters 9 and 10 specific suggestions are listed for activities that may be helpful in preparing for the new preschool experience.

WHY THIS BOOK IS IMPORTANT

You know your child and family best. Your partnership with professionals in deciding upon the kinds of services and assistance that optimally will help your family and your child is a critical part of successful intervention efforts. Parents, who in bygone days were told essentially to "institutionalize their child and forget they ever had the child at all," have now become the primary caregivers and the focal point for many of the services available to assist handicapped children. The extent to which parent involvement in early education is felt to be important is reflected in the fact that federal law (P.L. 94–142) mandates certain parent rights and responsibilities related to the education of handicapped children. (These rights and responsibilities are described in detail in Chapter 6.)

The information in this book may also be important to you because of your potential power as an advocate (one who speaks for another person in order to protect rights and interests) for your child. This is a critical time for handicapped children and for those who are concerned with their welfare. With cutbacks in federal funding a certainty, the future of your child rests on your ability to negotiate for services and programs at the local level. Although the focus of this book is on the preschool years, the framework adopted and the information included can be generalized to other ages. The decision-making process is indeed a process, and it is one that will continue throughout your child's life. *As the person who knows your child best and who has intimate knowledge about the needs of your family, you are in the best position to make sure that the educational decisions made are in the best interests of your child and family.*

WHAT DO YOU WANT FROM A PRESCHOOL EXPERIENCE?

The purpose of this section is to provide you with a rationale for preschool education and with strategies for identifying and clarifying both your needs and your child's needs. Much of the information in these chapters is based upon what parents who were interviewed in our research study on preschool services said were the factors influencing their own choice of a preschool. In Chapter 1 reasons are given why many parents consider preschool to be a very important experience for their handicapped child. Chapter 2 contains a description of child needs, and Chapter 3 includes a description of parent needs that may influence your choice of preschool programs. Parent and child needs are not always so easily separated. They are frequently intertwined in subtle and complicated ways. (The interaction of these needs is addressed more completely in Chapter 3.) There may be times when there is no preschool choice in which *both* parent needs and child needs can be met. For exam-

ple, a mother may feel that her bright and physically handicapped four-year-old would benefit from the type of exposure
he or she would get in a regular preschool program with nonhandicapped children. At the same time this mother may work
full-time and need all-day care for her child. She may find that
the regular preschools in her community are half-day programs
and that finding afternoon daycare for her child is difficult because of his or her handicap. The developmental center serving
only handicapped children has an all-day program that would
meet the mother's needs for daycare, but she feels this program
is too specialized for her child. Here is a case in which parent
and child needs are incompatible. In these cases hard choices
and compromises must be made.

Chapter 1

WHY SHOULD YOU CONSIDER PRESCHOOL FOR YOUR CHILD?

THE IMPORTANCE OF EARLY INTERVENTION

The preschool years are the most important years of learning in a child's life, according to a commonly accepted theory of early child development. In the case of handicapped children, growth and development may be delayed. Research has shown that intervention beginning in the early years, the years of rapid growth and development, can reduce the effects of a handicapping condition and can do so more effectively than intervention beginning later in a child's life.

Studies have consistently reported greater gains in developmental skills by handicapped children attending early intervention programs than by handicapped children who do not have this early education experience. The mother of a six-year-old with developmental delays comments:

If we had found an appropriate preschool for our daughter when she was younger, then she might not be as far behind as she is now. She didn't get help at the time that she needed it most. Most parents are not teachers. We're parents. If we wanted to teach, we would all be in the teaching profession. We do not have the

knowledge and the materials available to us to know
exactly how to teach a child who is delayed and
impaired. We need professionals to help us, and, most
importantly, to help our children.

More information on the contributions of early intervention to the development of handicapped children may be found in the resource section.

DEMANDS ON YOUR TIME
AND INCREASED RESPONSIBILITIES

Your child's special needs undoubtedly are having a significant impact on your life. Routine caregiving tasks, such as feeding, toileting, and dressing, may be made more difficult by delays in the development of your child's skills in self-care. These delays probably mean that your child is more dependent upon you for help and assistance in routine tasks of living and communicating. At an age at which many children are able to feed, dress, and go to the bathroom themselves, your child may require that much of your time be spent assisting with these tasks. A father of a five-year-old multiply handicapped child describes these needs as follows:

Our household routine is like a three-ring circus in the
mornings. Nancy and I both have to be at work at 8:00.
Because Megan is totally dependent on us, often we feel
like we've put in a full day of effort before we even
arrive at our jobs. I wake Megan and put her on the
potty and then I get dressed. Nancy bathes Megan and
dresses her while I prepare breakfast. Then I feed Megan
and brush her teeth while Nancy dresses. We are all
under stress, because Megan has never slept through the
night. It is hard to keep up such a busy routine when we
desperately need sleep.

Delays in your child's speech and language development may mean that you must spend a great deal of time interpreting your child's language to other people or struggling to understand what your child is saying. The mother of a hearing-impaired preschooler makes this comment:

It was really a bad time. Jason was having tantrums all of the time at home. He would go to the cabinet for something he wanted and point. I would hand him one object, and if that wasn't the one he wanted, then I would hand him another. Usually that wasn't the right one either. By the time I finally got what he wanted, he was so frustrated that he wouldn't want it anymore. He would just kick and yell. Then I would go to my room and kick and yell and sometimes say "Don't bother me anymore!" He really became a behavior problem because he couldn't communicate with us, and we couldn't communicate with him.

You probably have been told or may have read that it is up to you to stimulate your child in areas of delay. This can add up to additional demands on your time and additional responsibilities associated with educating your handicapped child. Parents of young handicapped children often feel that there is constant pressure on them to work with their child. The mother of a preschooler with spina bifida shares her thoughts about the difference she felt between parental responsibilities for her nonhandicapped son and for her handicapped son:

You take a lot for granted and tend to take things easier when there's no problem, but I think you always are going to feel more pressure if your little one is handicapped—there's no way around it. When you get a little one that doesn't do anything until you're the catalyst, it almost becomes an obsession because you feel like he'll be sitting there, and you know that either you could sew or you could get him to learn his "k" sounds.

Often parents feel what this mother expressed: it is difficult to take a break from the task of educating, stimulating, and encouraging a child with learning delays. Often professionals unknowingly encourage these feelings by requesting that parents take on demanding home stimulation programs, or perhaps each specialist seen by the child suggests a few exercises or tasks to be done at home, until the list becomes lengthy, and in some cases unmanageable. A mother of a severely retarded child describes some of the home interventions she is involved in:

We are working on a feeding program with Rod at breakfast and dinner. His teacher and occupational therapist set up the program and they use it at lunch. His progress is slow, but in the long run I am committed to helping him do as much as he possibly can for himself. The major problem for me right now is that it takes Rod almost one hour to eat each meal. This creates a real dilemma, because it cuts into my time for my three other children. We also try to set aside about 20 minutes each evening, and more on weekends, to help him learn to use his walker.

Many home training programs are very beneficial. We are not questioning their value at all. The point to be made is that you may want, and should be able, to receive assistance with the very important task of educating your child. Having professional help with these educational responsibilities may give you and your child more time to have fun together. Being able to relax, while knowing that someone else is working with your child on forming the "k" sound, may be the best form of therapy for you and your child. The single parent of a daughter with cerebral palsy offers her views on the need for some relaxation time at home:

I work full-time. When I get home in the afternoon, I'm tired and I have to fix dinner. Sally has been in a situation all day where she's had someone telling her she has to work on this and that. I don't feel like she's ready for more education at night. I think it's time for fun and enjoying Mommy for awhile. Plus, I don't think that children learn as well from their parents on some tasks that are particularly difficult. Parents tend to want to do the work for their children rather than watch them suffer. I'm that way when she goes to the physical therapist. The therapist will want to see what she can do and will tell her to take off her shirt. When she starts having trouble, I want to go over and help her, rather than really testing her to her limits.

Sondra Diamond,[1] a physically handicapped adult, addresses the importance of relaxation time in a chapter she wrote about growing up with her family. After years of being corrected and receiving therapy at home, she finally unleashed a tirade of angry feelings toward her well-meaning parents: "I'm just a kid! You can't therapize me all the time! I get enough therapy in school every day! I don't think about my handicap all the time like you do!"

The message here is clear: "Think of me as a child first. Let me be that at home and let other people concentrate on my disabilities." Finding those "other people," professionals whom you can trust to do a good job, is a major task for you.

INTEGRATING FAMILY NEEDS WITH YOUR CHILD'S NEEDS

The impact of your child's delay on you has been described in terms of demands on your time and increased responsibilities. However, there are other intense feelings experienced by the parents of a handicapped child. Eloquent accounts by parents of the fear, sorrow, exhaustion, anger, loneliness, and guilt associated with parenting a handicapped child are available in books. (See the resource section for references.) A mother of a mentally retarded child expresses some of these feelings:[2]

Every day I looked for Jennie to smile a little, to perhaps start turning, to squirm more in her crib. She was fussy, colicky, and she had trouble moving her bowels, but all of these things I could overlook. I was deeply distressed because what I was expecting to see as developmental landmarks were not appearing. In an attempt to try to get me away from my problem, my husband took me on a convention trip with him to Toronto. On that long drive through the mountains of New York State and

---

[1] Diamond, S. 1981. Growing up with parents of a handicapped child: A handicapped person's perspective. In: J.L. Paul (ed.), *Understanding and Working with Parents of Children with Special Needs.* Holt, Rinehart & Winston, Inc., New York.

[2] Ziskin, L. 1978. The story of Jennie. In: A.P. Turnbull and H.R. Turnbull (eds.), *Parents Speak Out: Views from the Other Side of the Two-way Mirror,* pp. 73–75. Charles E. Merrill Publishing Co., Columbus, OH.

Canada, I remember feeling that I had become a completely different person. I felt my ego had been wiped out. My superego with all its guilts had become the most prominent part of my personality and I had completely lost my self-esteem. I felt I was nobody. Any credits of self-worth that I could give myself from any of my personal endeavors meant nothing. Graduating from college and from a first-rate medical school, surviving an internship, practicing medicine, and having two beautiful sons and a good marriage counted for nil. All I knew at this point was that I was the mother of an abnormal and most likely retarded child.

Such accounts make it clear that one child's disability reshapes each family member's life in unexpected ways, and that each family develops unique ways of coping with the stress involved. Professionals play a big part in the lives of handicapped people and their families. One of the important ways that professionals can help families is by providing emotional support. Again, an important task for parents is finding professionals who can do this. The staffmembers of early intervention or preschool programs are in a position to provide you with needed support. In addition, they should be able to help you find others who can also do this—either other parents of handicapped children, professionals, or childcare helpers. The same mother who felt such frustration also shares insights on her daughter's progress and the *positive* aspects of her daughter's influence on the family:

Jennie has learned to walk. She started walking when she was four years of age, and it was more than just her own accomplishment. The school helped, her brothers helped, and our housekeepers helped. Jennie climbs stairs, eats with silverware, sits at the table with us, and drinks by herself. Jennie is now nine, and we hope her next major achievement will be getting toilet trained. In return for our efforts, Jennie gives us love and a sense of patience. She makes us see that all people do not learn or progress at the same rapid rate. She makes us appreciate the gift of speech, the gift of communication.

*She makes us marvel that she communicates with us in
her own way. She communicates by going to where
things are, by going to the drawer where the cookies are,
by going to the refrigerator when she wants a drink, by
perking up when she sees her coat.*[3]

Finding services in your community for your preschool
handicapped child is important both for you and for your child's
future. The major challenge facing you as a parent is matching
the needs of your child and of your family with the preschool
programs available in your community. Many different types of
early intervention or preschool programs exist. Some will be
better than others in providing you and your child with the
support and assistance that you need. There are people in your
community who are able to help you with this decision—other
parents and professionals, such as school administrators and
teachers, social workers, and health-related persons. Ultimately,
however, you and your child will be the persons most affected
by the decision. Also, with your intimate knowledge of the daily
needs of your family, you are in the best position to make an
informed decision about which program is best suited for your
situation.

---

[3] Ziskin, L. 1978. The story of Jennie. In: A.P. Turnbull and H.R. Turnbull (eds.),
Parents Speak Out: Views from the Other Side of the Two-way Mirror. p. 78.
Charles E. Merrill Publishing Co., Columbus, OH.

Chapter 2

WHAT DOES YOUR CHILD NEED FROM A PRESCHOOL?

DETERMINING YOUR CHILD'S NEEDS

When reviewing your child's needs, it is important to first consider what your child can and cannot do in terms of specific skills and developmental areas. It is also important to think about the kind of activities or special help you feel would benefit your child. This is not an easy task. As one parent states:

I know my child well and am aware of his basic needs, but I do not know how to translate this into academic terminology. I do not know what are appropriate long-term and short-term goals for my child. Sometimes I assume that he cannot or should not be working on a skill, then later I discover that he could have or should have accomplished that. My basic question is this: How do I continually discover what goals my child should be working on and how do I figure out the best ways to help him reach those goals?

GETTING INFORMATION FROM PROFESSIONALS

Seeking professional opinions is one way of gathering information about what your child needs. Each professional who sees your child will interpret your child's needs according to his or her own particular specialty area. For instance, a doctor may evaluate a child with cerebral palsy and report a hopeless prognosis, because, from the doctor's perspective, there is no cure for the condition. An education specialist assessing the same child would offer a different view. Based upon an evaluation of the child's cognitive abilities and learning style, this person could structure an individualized education program (IEP) with a good prognosis for success. A physical therapist evaluating the same child would provide a third perspective. After assessing various factors, such as the child's trunk and head control and muscle tone, this person would devise a therapy program with its own set of criteria for success. Unfortunately, there is no one professional who will be able to evaluate your child from all perspectives. As a parent you may need to sort out what various professionals have told you and to coordinate a combination of therapies and programs that best meet your child's needs. The father of a blind child relates his experience:

You have to use your instinct with professionals. They don't automatically communicate with each other. We feel like we've had to teach them how to work together. The most fruitful thing we've done is to schedule sessions in which our occupational therapist, our pediatrician, the audiologist, and the preschool teacher meet together. This is the only way to coordinate services.

By bringing professionals together, it may be possible to avoid or to resolve some of the dilemmas reported by parents in trying to figure out what their child's most pressing needs are and how to help them best. One mother states:

With Annie there have been such big questions from the very beginning. We knew there was a visual impairment but we were so unsure about her other problems. In her infant program the master teacher was a specialist on visual impairments, so those needs were met very well. In her next program they said that her developmental delays were a bigger problem than her vision, so they honed in on those. I felt that what she really needed

*from the beginning was help in both areas. Both
programs were good in one area but each seemed to
ignore a part of Annie that needed help. Now I wish I
had insisted that each teacher work with her in both
areas and get help from other specialists when they
didn't know what to do.*

The father of a child with cerebral palsy recounts a similar
dilemma:

*The physical therapist told us that Matt needed to be
continually repositioned in order to try to prevent
spasticity. That meant that throughout the day he had to
be changed from a standing board to a corner chair. It
takes about 15 minutes just to get him from one of these
positions to another. Meanwhile Matt's teacher told us
that Matt learned best when sitting up. What was best?
We could move him from position to position, knowing
that precious little time could be spent on learning
tasks, or we could leave him in a sitting position,
knowing that he might end up being shaped like a chair,
but at least he might be a smart "chair."*

Perhaps the worst situation for parents is when professionals have no answers. Helen Harrison[4] recounts her own
search for help:

*When we first consulted developmental specialists, we
hoped for answers about Edward's condition and
suggestions for helping him. What we got instead was
confusion. Yes, Edward was ready for toilet training. No,
he wasn't. Yes, heel cord surgery would help him walk
better. No, that was the worst thing we could do. We soon
learned that there was no right answer to any question
about Edward's care and upbringing. We began to rely
more and more on our own judgment. We continued to
seek professional insight, but we tried to find doctors
and therapists with whom we felt compatible; people
whose advice made sense to us.*

---

[4] Harrison, H. 1983. *The Premature Baby Book: A Parents' Guide to Coping
and Caring in the First Years.* St. Martin's Press, New York.

As parents it is important to recognize that no book and no one person can perfectly describe a child's needs. This is a difficult, ongoing process, frequently characterized by conflicting opinions and difficult decisions about where to focus resources and time.

THINKING ABOUT YOUR CHILD IN A SYSTEMATIC WAY

You know your child better than anyone else does. You know what your child can or cannot do on a daily basis, likes and dislikes, and what kinds of things motivate the child to learn. In talking with professionals, you may find it helpful to be able to translate what you know into the language frequently used by educators. Table 2.1 is provided to help you do this. In the left column of the table are examples of specific skills or tasks you might want your child to learn, in the middle column is a general term for describing those skills, and in the right column is the educational term frequently used to describe those skills.

You also are well aware of what you want your child to accomplish that would make life easier for you at home. When the child learns to eat independently and becomes toilet trained, it certainly has a far more beneficial effect on the entire family than does his or her mastering a peg board. The father of a child with cerebral palsy makes this comment about his son's educational goals:

There is so much that Tim needs and so many things that need to be worked on. What is most *important? We have to make sure that what he's learning is as practical as possible. For instance, instead of teaching him to match shapes with puzzle pieces, we have used cut-out shapes of plates, forks, spoons, and napkins. Essentially we have taught him how to set a table. There is just not enough time for these kids to waste it on meaningless activities. We get together with the occupational therapist and try to be as creative as possible.*

As a way of thinking about what you want your child to learn now, you might ask yourself:

Table 2.1. Skills you may want your child to learn translated into terms educators may use

Examples of specific skills or activities you may want your child to master	General terms	Educators' term
Learning new words, talking in sentences, learning sign language	Talking/listening/communicating	Language development
Crawling, standing, sitting, improving head control, walking, hopping, climbing, using a walker, stringing beads, grasping objects	Moving/coordinating	Motor development
Drinking from a cup, dressing, putting on shoes, washing hands, combing hair, learning to use the toilet	Taking care of oneself	Self-help skills
Sharing, taking turns, helping a friend, playing with other children, recognizing familiar faces	Getting along with others	Social development
Leaving parents, asking for what one wants, standing up for oneself	Independence and ability to adjust to different types of situations	Adaptive behavior
Making positive comments about oneself, having a sense of being an important and lovable person, feeling relaxed and secure in familiar surroundings, having a basic acceptance of oneself	Feeling good about oneself	Self-concept
Looking at pictures in a book, recognizing letters, counting objects	Reading and math skills	Cognitive/pre-academic skills

1. What three skills has my child recently learned or accomplished?
2. What three skills is my child working on learning now?
3. What three skills would I most like my child to learn within the next six months?

These three questions are included in Table 2.2, which you can complete by using the information in Table 2.1 as a guide.

In Column A of Table 2.2, write down the specific skills (e.g., learning new words, using a spoon, and taking turns) that your child has recently learned, is working on now, and that you would like for the child to learn in the near future. You may want to refer to the lists of skills in the left column of Table 2.1 as you work on this. The list of skills in Table 2.1 is far from exhaustive; therefore, you should include skills in Table 2.2 (other than those listed in Table 2.1) that are relevant for your child. In Column B of Table 2.2 you can begin to associate your child's specific skills with the actual terms that educators use. The right column of Table 2.1 may be a helpful reference as you complete Column B.

If you are having trouble answering the questions on the table, then perhaps you need more information about your child. One approach is to talk about the questions with someone else (a professional, friend, relative, or neighbor) who knows your child. Another approach is to step back and closely observe your child. Excellent suggestions for ways systematically to observe your child in order to gather facts are available in *Negotiating the Special Education Maze* by Anderson et al. (See the resource section for a description of this book.)

PROGRAM CHARACTERISTICS IMPORTANT IN HELPING YOUR CHILD TO MAKE PROGRESS IN SKILL AREAS

You may also think about your child's needs in terms of specific services, people, and program characteristics that you think would be helpful in promoting your child's skill development and learning.

Table 2.2. Chart of your child's skill development

Questions	Column A Specific skills	Column B Educators' terms
1) What three skills has your child recently learned or accomplished?	a) b) c)	a) b) c)
2) What three skills is your child working on learning now?	a) b) c)	a) b) c)
3) What three skills would you most like your child to learn within the next six months?	a) b) c)	a) b) c)

Table adapted from Anderson, W., Chitwood, S., and Hayden, D. 1981. *Negotiating the Special Education Maze.* Spectrum Books, Englewood Cliffs, NJ.

Teacher Qualifications and Attitudes

Generally speaking, the most important part of your child's pre-school is the teachers who work with your child and arrange your child's environment. A competent preschool teacher should be: warm and responsive with children; should encourage developmental growth; should be respectful of individual needs and feel comfortable working with handicapped children; should be able to cope with the demands of working with groups of children; and should be consistent and fair in disciplining the children.

Individualized Instruction

A large number of children combined with a small number of teachers may pose problems for children who learn best with individualized instruction. Most children, handicapped and nonhandicapped alike, benefit from instruction that is specifically tailored to their needs.

Keeping Track of the Child's Progress and Development

It is important for you to consider how can you be sure that your child's growth and development are being promoted in a preschool program. Having carefully thought about your child's needs and the ways in which those needs can be met, you should seek information throughout the year about your child's progress in various areas of development.

Related Support Services

Some preschools, especially those designed for handicapped children, have access to many related services, such as vision consultants, speech and physical therapists, and counselors. Others may offer few, if any, such services. If you think your child could benefit from these related services, it is important that you inquire about this preschool feature. It may also be important to look beyond the mere presence or absence of such related services, and to consider the staff's willingness and ability to locate and to coordinate the related services your child needs, if the preschool does not already have them.

The Arrangement of Space in the Preschool

Classroom space is an important dimension of a preschool program. In exploring their physical environment, children must sense their ability to navigate and to move freely. Furniture and equipment should be arranged so that children can identify traffic paths that they can use to get from one place to another. Bathrooms, stairs, and playgrounds must be adapted so that handicapped children can use these facilities with ease.

Children occasionally need the feeling of security found in physically small areas, where they may enjoy their solitude. It can be very demanding on children if they must spend all their time in large rooms with a number of other children. Small cubbyhole areas allow children to go off and experience the relative peace of investigating a new toy by themselves or with one or two friends. Large open spaces that are not arranged to provide these needed areas can be impersonal.

Emotional and Social Climate of the Preschool

The emotional and social climate of the preschool can largely influence your child's security and self-confidence. The responsiveness of your child's teacher and peer group is an important consideration.

Specific questions relating to each of these program characteristics are provided in Chapter 8 to help you when you are ready to visit preschools.

WHICH NEEDS CAN BE MET BEST IN PRESCHOOL SETTINGS?

Developing an idea about what your child's needs are should be the first step toward getting those needs met. Thinking about the preschool characteristics important in helping your child make progress is the second step. The third step is taking a look around you—at your neighborhood, your family, and your community—and thinking about other resources that might help your child. It may be unrealistic to expect that a preschool program will provide you with everything you need. A good idea at this point is to fine-tune your ideas of what you want from a preschool program and to figure out which of your needs can *only* be met in the preschool setting. This fine-tuning will help you to focus your attention on specific needs when you look at preschools in your community. If you have decided in advance what kinds of services or experiences you consider to be absolutely necessary components of a preschool program, then your search for an appropriate preschool can be made easier.

To help you think about your child's needs and the type of program in which those needs can be met best, Table 2.3 provides a summary of information. In the left column of this table are examples of needs your child might have. The next column lists various ways in which those needs could be met. In the third column are hypothetical community and family resources that might be available to help meet each child need. The last two columns contain hypothetical information to answer two questions: 1) "Can my child's needs be met adequately outside of a preschool experience?" and 2) "If not, what services or experiences do I expect the preschool to provide?"

A version of this table (Table 2.4.) with the last three columns left blank has been provided so that you may sketch in information relevant to your child and community. After completing this task, you should have a clearer idea about what you are looking for in a preschool experience for your child.

Table 2.3. Different needs your child may have and where and how these needs may be met

Child needs	Ways in which needs can be met	Community and family resources for meeting needs	Can this need be met adequately outside of preschool?	If not, what services or experiences does the family expect the preschool to provide?
Talking and listening skills	Being in an environment in which talking and listening are encouraged Having a speech therapist work with the child individually or in a small group Being around other children who have talking and listening skills and copying their language patterns	Talking and listening can be encouraged at home Family can afford to hire a speech therapist to work with the child; however, there are not children in the neighborhood to stimulate the child's use of language	No. The family may feel that it is just as important for the child to be around other children in order to improve talking and listening skills as it is to have speech therapy	Environment that encourages use of language Opportunities for the child to work with a speech therapist
Moving and coordinating	Opportunities to copy other children's movements and their use of toys, i.e., watching another child ride a tricycle or climb a jungle gym	Services of physical therapist are available at local hospital. Parents can afford and are willing to arrange this service privately	Yes. Parents feel that the services of a therapist are adequate for meeting the child's needs now	

Continued

Table 2.3—*Continued*

Child needs	Ways in which needs can be met	Community and family resources for meeting needs	Can this need be met adequately outside of preschool?	If not, what services or experiences does the family expect the preschool to provide?
	Physical therapy, such as special exercises to improve coordination and range of motion			
Taking care of oneself	Opportunities to copy other children

Being in an environment in which taking care of oneself is encouraged

Being taught specific skills involved in feeding and dressing, either individually or in a small group | The child may be encouraged at home to take care of self, but parents feel that the child needs help in mastering tasks involved in feeding and dressing | No. Parents know of no community resources that would help them teach their child various tasks, such as feeding and dressing self | Teachers with the time and skill to teach the child tasks involved in feeding and dressing self; services of an occupational therapist to work with the child or with the teacher on these tasks |

Getting along with others	Opportunities to be around other children	Child has no siblings and there are few children in neighborhood. Child attends church school class with other children	No. Church school class meets too infrequently	Opportunities to be around other children in setting where interactions are encouraged
Independence	Being exposed to different situations, being allowed to experience risks, i.e., situations that are different in some way and require some adjustment	Family takes child on trips and family outings. Child has been left with babysitters and relatives	No. Family feels child needs more experiences in larger groups of children	Situation as close to the real world as possible. Opportunities to learn to handle problem with other children
Feeling good about oneself	Being in environment in which individual differences are valued, where the child's strengths are recognized, where love and acceptance of the child is evident, and opportunities for success abound	Home environment and church school meet these criteria	No. Parents feel preschool setting must have these qualities to be acceptable	Staff who demonstrate acceptance of child, who value child's individual difference, who give child support for success, and who actively transmit these attitudes to other children in class through words and actions

Table 2.4. Chart on child's needs for parents to complete

Child needs	Ways in which needs can be met	Community and family resources for meeting needs	Can this need be met adequately outside of preschool?	If not, what services or experiences does the family expect the preschool to provide?
Talking and listening skills	Being in an environment in which talking and listening is encouraged			
	Having a speech therapist work with the child individually or in a small group			
	Being around other children who have talking and listening skills and copying their language patterns			
Moving and coordinating	Opportunities to copy other children's movements and their use of toys, i.e., watching another child ride a tricycle or climb a jungle gym			

Physical therapy, such as special exercises to improve coordination and range of motion

Taking care of oneself

Opportunities to copy other children

Being in an environment in which taking care of oneself is encouraged

Being taught specific skills involved in feeding and dressing, either individually or in a small group

Getting along with others

Opportunities to be around other children

Continued

Table 2.4—*Continued*

Child needs	Ways in which needs can be met	Community and family resources for meeting needs	Can this need be met adequately outside of preschool?	If not, what services or experiences does the family expect the preschool to provide?
Independence	Being exposed to different situations and being allowed to experience risks, i.e. situations that are different in some way and require some adjustment			
Feeling good about oneself	Being in an environment in which individual differences are valued, where the child's strengths are recognized, and where love and acceptance of the child is evident and opportunities for success abound			

Chapter 3

WHAT DOES YOUR FAMILY NEED FROM A PRESCHOOL?

Discussing parent and family needs is more difficult than discussing child needs. One cause of this difficulty is that accepted theories of child development map out expected areas of growth and development in children. Although the development of handicapped children may be delayed or erratic, the general areas of development in which growth and learning are expected to take place can still be described with a certain amount of confidence. There is no comparably acceptable theory of adult development. When families are concerned, the issue becomes even more complicated. Various intricate models and theories regarding family systems have been devised, but most people who have studied and analyzed the way families operate agree that families are unique and complicated systems and that each member of that system has a profound effect on every other member of that system. The recognition of this relationship is one of the reasons why laws, policies, and programs affecting handicapped children have broadened in focus to include families. The information in this chapter on family needs is based upon two underlying assumptions. One assumption is that the well-being of the child depends more upon the well-being of the family in which the child resides than it does upon a particular type of treatment for the child. In other words, the most effective program is the one that best meets the needs of the family as a whole. The other assumption is that each family's situation is unique. The combination of events experienced by your own family may create needs very different from those of other families you know.

The major purpose of this chapter is twofold. The first section is meant to stimulate you to think about your own particular circumstances, and to reinforce the idea that your needs and your child's needs are delicately intertwined. The second section focuses on the external environment and is designed to help you think about what kind of involvement you would like to have at your child's preschool.

DIFFERENT FAMILY NEEDS THAT YOU MIGHT BE EXPERIENCING

The Need for Professional Involvement So That You Can Take a Break from the Full-time Responsibilities of Educating Your Child

When most parents select a preschool, their primary concern is to find what is best for their child. Most parents have a strong need to know that their child is happy and is getting the best care available. Making a preschool selection based upon the child's best interests will obviously benefit the child. It may not be as obvious, however, how much and in what ways the right choice will benefit parents. Our research with parents indicates that having competent and kind professionals take over the education of their handicapped child for part of the day contributes to the ability of many parents to relax. Parents of young handicapped children often feel a tremendous amount of pressure to stimulate their child constantly. One mother, who is an elementary school teacher as well as a parent of a severely handicapped daughter, expresses the extent to which she feels the need to separate her roles as parent and as teacher of her young daughter:

I think you have to be removed as a parent from the teaching situation. Living with a handicapped child and trying to train the child by yourself is just about an impossibility. It's just that the constant supervision of a handicapped child really gets to you after a while. It's frustrating enough without having to teach them, too.

Another mother of a severely handicapped young girl describes her own realization that she could not devote herself entirely to her handicapped daughter and maintain her own sanity:

I have come to realize that somebody is going to have to take care of Toni other than myself. I have listened to mothers in the Infant Group (mothers' support group) and what they say is how I used to feel: "I produced this child, this defective child, and I've got to take care of her." I don't know if it's guilt or what. But finally I realized that if anything happens to me, if I run myself down, then what's going to happen? Who's going to take care of Toni? So I said, "I'd better think about me. I better get this act together right here and now, because suppose I crack up over this? I'm not going to be competent to take care of Toni, Rachel, my other daughter, or James, my husband." So that's when I first decided that I should take her out and let somebody else help with her. It was kind of rough at first, but I began to see the benefits. I learned to trust the people working with her and to have confidence in them.

This last statement illustrates an important point: parents are not willing to turn their child over to just anybody. A very important part of being able to relax is knowing that the people working with your child are competent and caring.

One mother, who is a nurse by training, has a son with spina bifida. She expresses her feelings in this way:

You've got to have a staff that is smarter than you when it comes to your child's handicap. I'm not a genius; I mean, my background is giving enemas. But you've got to know that the people that are teaching your child know their stuff. Now I drop off Sam in the morning and I feel like, whew, people more competent than I are taking care of him, and that's a great feeling.

The mother of a hearing-impaired child describes more fully how the impact of letting competent professionals take over her child's education affected her life:

I'm a different person. There were times when I would feel like I couldn't handle him anymore. I would think, "I'm going to pack my bags and walk completely out of here." But he's had some successes and I think that's what we really feel good about. I quit working, but it wasn't because John needed me. I stopped because I didn't like the job situation. And I was finally able to separate what I needed to do for myself from John's needs. Because I felt like John was o.k. I know what he does in the morning and what he's doing in the afternoon. I know where he is, and I know what's going on. I didn't have the feeling any longer that I had to supplement what was going on during the day, because I felt he was getting what he needed.

The important point is that competent, trustworthy, and kind teachers are crucial, not only for the child, but also for the parents.

Logistical Concerns, or Practical Needs

Practical considerations, such as the cost of a program, the convenience of the program (how close is it to your home, whether transportation is provided), and the need for daycare, may enter into your selection of a preschool. These issues are frequently faced by parents whether or not their child is handicapped. There are ways, however, in which having a handicapped child may limit your options. Finding daycare is an example of a possible hindrance. The mother of a young child with cerebral palsy describes how her return to work part-time was thwarted by her inability to find daycare for her handicapped daughter: "I called various daycare centers, and the minute I told them that my daughter was handicapped they said, 'Well, we don't have the staff available, we don't have the facilities, and we can't take your child.' I heard this over and over again." This mother did not return to work until she enrolled her daughter in a preschool program that included an extended-day component.

The Need for Opportunities To Be Directly Involved with Your Child's Program

Most families like to maintain contact with their child's pre-school in some way. Some family members like having more than contact; they like participating in activities designed especially for them. Our research has indicated that there is tremendous variability among parents' needs and preferences concerning the amount and type of involvement that they have in their child's preschool program. The types of involvement considered in this section include informal contact with teachers, counseling, training, and contact with other parents of handicapped children.

Informal but Frequent Contact with Your Child's Teacher Based upon our research, the type of involvement activity most preferred by the majority of parents is informal contact with teachers. This preference seems very much related to the need to know that competent and caring teachers are working with your child. Parents say that they liked these contacts because they were frequent (drop-off and pick-up times were thought to provide excellent opportunities to talk with teachers), and information could be shared between parents and teachers in a give-and-take fashion. It seems that trust and confidence grow from having this sort of relationship with your child's teachers.

The following description, given by the mother of a hearing-impaired preschooler concerning her relationship with her child's teachers, illustrates how important the parent-professional relationship can be:

In a way, they [the child's teachers] became a substitute family. I could tell them in the morning what had happened at home the night before; and at the end of the day they would tell me what John [her handicapped son] had done that day. There's a special attitude: "We care about you as parents, and even though we're here to work with your child, you're involved, and we want to work with you." So I never felt like I was shut out, or that they would do anything that I was not interested in having them do.

A father makes this comment about the staff at his daughter's preschool: "We knew they were doing what needed to be done. They were doing it the way we asked them to do it. They always let us know how Cindy was progressing."

Family Counseling   Tremendous strain often accompanies parenting a handicapped child. The experiences of many parents make it clear that some professional contacts are more likely to *increase* the strain than to relieve it. Helen Harrison describes her own experiences as follows:

Unfortunately, the "helping" professionals (with a few wonderful exceptions) did little to help us or our son. As parents of a high-risk baby, we were often treated as specimens of pathology, rather than as normal people coping with a difficult situation. At a clinic appointment, if Alfred held Edward while I talked to the doctor (our usual roles, because I was the medical one in the family), I was labeled a "non-nurturing" mother. If I took Edward to a therapist by myself, I was solemnly questioned about whether the father was involved. One time a doctor who had kept the three of us waiting for an hour and a half noted our agitation and suggested that we receive psychological counseling to help us adjust to parenting a handicapped child. We had to bite our tongues to keep from offering the countersuggestion that counseling might also help the good doctor keep to his schedule.[5]

Ken Yockey, the father of a mentally retarded daughter, talks about what it's like to be labeled by professionals as a parent who "can't cope with" or "has a difficult time accepting" his or her child's mental retardation. From Ken's perspective, once the original psychologist who evaluated their child made the judgement that his wife Barb was having a difficult time accepting the mental retardation, succeeding psychologists (who had access to this report) reached the same conclusions. The following

---

[5] Harrison, H. 1983. *The Premature Baby Book: A Parents' Guide to Coping and Caring in the First Years.* St. Martin's Press, New York.

excerpt is his reaction to this situation, as described in the book *We Have Been There:*[6]

During the previous 18 months, Barb had spent a great deal of time and energy running all over the county investigating programs for handicapped children, talking with other parents, learning about mental retardation, and driving Debbie to and from her preschool program five days a week. She joined the County Association for Retarded Children (now "for Retarded Citizens") and started going to meetings. In short her whole lifestyle had been changed almost overnight, and her priorities had been completely rearranged. She even tried to get me to go with her to the association's meetings, but I spent most of my time working and the rest of the time trying not to think about my daughter's problem. I honestly can't imagine how Barb could have accepted Debbie's mental retardation any better, but then the psychologist never asked Barb what she had been doing with her life for the past year and one-half. Anyone could bet that the second psychologist was prejudiced by the first psychologist's report, which had been supplied to the school district.

The need for support for families is obvious. What kind of support will be most helpful and how you can find it depends upon your own situation. One of the options that you might want to consider is counseling. This could either be a formal arrangement with a professional, such as a psychiatrist, social worker, or psychologist, or an informal arrangement with one of the staff members of your child's program or with another parent. The ideal situation, according to one mother, is to find a trained counselor who is also the parent of a handicapped child. An early intervention program in California is developing a unique counseling service for parents. Each family in their program would have access to a team of counselors comprised of

---

[6] Yockey, K. 1983. Playing blocks with psychologists. In: T. Dougan, L. Isbell, and P. Vyas (eds.), *We Have Been There: A Guidebook for Parents of People with Mental Retardation.* Abingdon Press, Nashville, TN.

both a parent of an older handicapped child and a professional counselor. Most preschool programs can help you find some kind of counseling if you want it.

Training for Family Members Parents of young handicapped children, as the primary decision makers and caregivers, are expected to function effectively in many roles that require considerable information and skill. Parents are often expected to master the knowledge of complicated laws, an understanding of complex educational systems, information on the nature of their child's handicapping condition, and skills for managing and teaching their child. In addition, some programs expect parents to conduct ongoing therapy programs with their child at home. You should find out what programs the preschools in your community have for training family members. Helen Harrison makes these observations about her idea of a good parent program: "A good therapy program *helps the parents.* It gives them moral support, practical advice on caregiving, feedback on their child's progress, and suggestions for helpful activities that they can enjoy together with the child."[7] She has this warning about parent therapy programs:

When concerned parents set out to help their child, they naturally want to make every possible effort. But too great an emphasis on remedial activities can be counterproductive. The parents may focus so intently on the child's problems that they lose sight of the child himself and his normal emotional needs. They may spend countless hours on therapy, doing lots of things to their child but not much with him. While chauffering their child from one special program to the next, they may leave the child with little time alone to practice skills or just to play and have fun. For the child's sake, the parents' sake, and the sake of the other children in the family, therapy should be integrated as unobtrusively as possible into the family's normal routine. Each family member should share in the inevitable extra work so that no one person becomes overburdened. Each family member, including the child

---

[7] Harrison, H. 1983. *The Premature Baby Book: A Parents' Guide to Coping and Caring in the First Years.* St. Martin's Press, New York.

with the problem, should have time for himself for fun and recreation.

In looking at preschool programs you should consider what kinds of training opportunities they can offer you, and what expectations they have about your participation in your child's program, both in the classroom and at home.

Contact with Other Parents of Handicapped Children Talking with other parents who share similar concerns and interests has been described by some parents as being tremendously support-ive. A mother offers her views on why such contact is helpful:

If I dealt only with parents of normal children, I would be a crazy person. I need a support group of people who really understand what it is to have a handicapped child, who wonder not only how to handle the child at age 3 or 4, but also think ahead and wonder and worry about what to do when the child becomes an adult at ages 20 and 35.

Some programs have ongoing support groups like the ones just described. Other programs that do not have structured groups may offer other opportunities, such as potluck suppers, discussion groups, or parent workdays, for parents to get to-gether informally. One parent, who found no support group in his child's program, successfully got one started in the commu-nity. He offers some advice for those who might want to do the same:

Locating other parents of handicapped children in the community can be a problem. Confidentiality laws have forbidden programs from releasing the names of children enrolled. Do not let this discourage you. Let these programs distribute the initial information about support groups to parents; in most cases, they are glad to do so.

ATTITUDES TOWARD PARENT INVOLVEMENT THAT YOU MIGHT FIND IN DIFFERENT PRESCHOOLS

Most preschool programs have responded to the growing aware-ness of the importance of families by developing programs or sets of activities specifically for parents. One researcher, who conducted a survey of preschool programs for handicapped children around the country, identified 34 different types of activities that had been developed for parents in these programs. From one perspective, this information is encouraging; it suggests that parents have a wide variety of services and activities to help them in their parenting role. However, from another viewpoint the information from this survey is discouraging, because it indicated that providing services and activities for parents based upon the parents' *individual needs and preferences* is not a top priority for professionals. To get parents involved, programs often develop a prescribed set of parent activities. These activities might include opportunities to assist in the classroom, opportunities to assist outside of the classroom (i.e., fund raising, volunteering in the office, or driving on field trips), advisory board membership, parent-training workshops, parent support groups, and parent-teacher conferences. The staffmembers who set up these activities often expect that "interested and concerned" parents will participate in as many activities as possible.

However, this approach to involving parents may lead to problems, both for professionals and for parents. This method ignores the fact that parents of handicapped children are a heterogeneous rather than a homogeneous group, with different degrees of capability, time, energy, and interest in being involved with their children's educational programs. Parents may feel guilty if they do not have the time or the interest to participate in a prescribed set of activities set up by their child's teachers. The professionals who took the time and energy to arrange the activities may feel frustrated and unappreciated when parents do not participate. Misunderstanding and alienation on all sides may result.

An alternative approach to involving parents is to develop programs that are responsive to the individual needs and preferences of families. For several reasons, this approach is a more successful one.

The importance of individualizing the program to suit the child is an accepted principle in most programs—why not do the same for families? Instead of presenting all the parents with a set of activities in which they "ought to" participate, programs should start with an assessment of families' needs, preferences, and expectations concerning the preschool program. Programs that are individualized for the parents should recognize certain premises.

Family Structures Have Changed

Parent involvement activities frequently are focused on mothers and are offered during the morning and afternoon hours, a time that is usually inconvenient for parents employed outside the home. Forty-eight percent of preschool children have mothers working or looking for work.[8] Furthermore, a large increase in the number of young children living in single-parent homes can be expected because of the high divorce rate.

These changes in family structures have implications for preschool programs. Parent services and activities should be offered at times when both mothers and fathers employed outside the home and single parents can be involved. Fathers, who have traditionally been ignored by those studying the effects of parenting a handicapped child, are frequently overlooked when parent programs are planned. Some fathers may feel isolated from their families as a result. One mother relates her experience:

I was in the mother's group and got really close to everyone there. That's where I poured out my heart. But to tell you the truth, I sometimes don't know what my husband is really thinking about our son's handicap. I know he's deeply hurt, but he won't really talk about it. I think he's trying to protect me by being strong himself, but I can't help but wish he had a support group, someone other than me so he could really unburden himself.

A father talks about his feelings of isolation from his colleagues at work:

I have found that I don't have anyone to talk to about Bob except for my wife, Jean. I have a problem

---

[8] Report on Preschool Education. 1982. 14(10):5.

expressing my feelings; I think most men do. This sounds biased, but at work I notice that most men don't talk about their problems. I spend all day at work, and it would really help if I could talk to people there, but I don't think it would be acceptable.

Research has shown that fathers typically take on a "play-making" role when interacting with their normally developing children. What happens when a child is delayed in developing play skills? Are fathers able to take on a new role and carry out the caregiving tasks usually done by mothers? Or do fathers become isolated, unable to function in their normal role and unable to make the switch to a nontraditional role? A father of a severely handicapped preschooler describes his own situation: "I wonder if I should be doing more. Trish, my wife, has taken on the major portion of the problem. She has him all day except when he goes to the Infant Program, and then she drives 15 miles to take him there. I wish there were some way I could help more." Programs should be able to offer emotional support to fathers and should offer them assistance in dealing with the shift to new roles demanded by the special needs of a handicapped child.

Needs of Other Family Members Are Recognized

A program with an individualized approach should recognize that siblings of handicapped children and members of the extended family, such as grandparents, aunts, and uncles, might need and want support from preschool programs. Grandparents can be key members of a family, yet the grief they experience and the misunderstandings they might have about a handicapped grandchild are often overlooked by professionals. This can cause problems for all family members. One mother with a handicapped child explains:

I dreaded my mother-in-law's visits. Even though Lisa clearly had Down's syndrome, her grandmother refused to believe anything was wrong. She constantly was asking if we had gotten another opinion, because she thought all of the previous doctors were wrong. She also continually asked if I were spending enough time with Lisa, as if this might be the cause of her problems. After a weekend of that, I was a wreck.

Brothers and sisters inevitably are affected by having a handicapped sibling. From an adult perspective, Marge Helsel[9] recalls some of her early reactions to her multiply handicapped brother:

I cannot pinpoint exactly the time or the circumstance when I first became aware of Robin's handicaps. Several incidents come to mind, all of which occurred around the time I was eleven years old. One involved a trip to the shoe store where Robin was to be fitted for orthopedic shoes; another, a trip to the town near our country home for dinner at the YMCA. On both of these occasions, I can remember being acutely embarrassed by the ill-concealed stares our family received as we entered pushing Robin in his wheelchair. I was certain that everyone was looking at my brother with his obvious handicap and then wondering what was wrong with the rest of us. As a result of the feelings aroused in me by those occurrences, I began to refuse to go out to dinner or shopping with my family and took precautions to avoid being seen on the street or in the yard with Robin.

These avoidance procedures on my part were not taken without an accompanying sense of guilt. I knew that it was wrong for me to be ashamed of my brother. I loved Robin dearly and realized that the opinions (real or imagined) of others should have had no bearing on my relationship with him. Professional counseling or a peer support group with other siblings of handicapped youngsters might be useful in helping brothers and sisters understand these feelings and experiences. Looking back, I think I would have benefited from some counseling during this period. As an adult, I now realize

---

[9] Helsel, E. 1978. The Helsel's story of Robin. In: A.P. Turnbull and H.R. Turnbull (eds.), *Parents Speak Out: Views from the Other Side of the Two-way Mirror,* pp. 110–111. Charles E. Merrill Publishing Co., Columbus, OH.

that my reactions to Robin's handicaps were not unusual, but I certainly did not know this at the time. It would have helped me to be able to talk with an adult other than my mother or father about the feelings I was experiencing because I think it would be extremely difficult for any youngster to admit point-blank to her parents that she is embarrassed by her brother. I believe most children growing up in a society that places a great deal of emphasis on so-called normalcy come to a point when they are ashamed of, or even outright reject, a disabled sibling. It is at this time that they should be given a concise explanation of the disability (i.e., what it is, why it happened, and the prognosis), be permitted the opportunity of exploring their feelings about their sibling, and, if necessary, be given some guidance in problem solving and in coping skills to help them deal with their feelings in a constructive manner.

Many preschool programs are beginning to expand the notion of parent support to one of family support.

Finally, in the area of family needs, professionals should recognize the extent to which a therapy program directed toward a handicapped child may impinge on other family members. If parents are expected to be involved with their handicapped child's program to the extent that they don't have time for PTA, Cub Scouts, and activities in which their normal child participates, then the program is not going to be helpful to the family.

Families' Needs Change over Time

An individualized parent program recognizes that families' needs and preferences evolve over time. A parent activity might have worked successfully with a parent or group of parents one year, but may not offer those same parents what they need the next year.

One mother expressed her changing sentiments toward a mother's support group provided by her child's program as follows: "It [the mother's group] was good at that time, and I think

I'll always have a feeling for those mothers because we got so close, but I don't miss it now. I don't feel the need for it. I may when my child gets older and there are more problems."

Another mother, who had been heavily involved in advocacy work and had participated in a mother's group in the past, describes the change in her attitudes with this comment:

When our son was first born we really got involved, and it was tremendously beneficial. But now I just want to draw back and make sure that this little guy gets attention at home. When you're putting in so much time that your family is no longer benefiting, then it's time to quit and let somebody else to do it. That's the point we reached.

The need to withdraw from program involvement in order to have more time with the family illustrates the importance of making a distinction between involvement with the program and involvement with the child. Too often parent programs become an end in themselves, rather than a means of helping parents cope in their own unique way with life with their handicapped child. When investigating what a preschool program can offer you as a parent, the most important criterion should be the staff's attention to family needs, their validation of those needs, and the flexibility they exhibit in planning to meet those needs.

WHICH OF YOUR FAMILY'S NEEDS CAN BE MET BEST IN A PRESCHOOL?

Developing an accurate idea about your family's needs is one of the first steps in getting those needs met. Locating a program receptive to your family's needs and flexible in their approach toward parent involvement is the second important step. The third step is to look within your community for different programs and other ways in which those needs might be met.

A table similar to the one on child needs in the last chapter has been provided to help you as you consider your family's needs. In Column 1 are examples of needs you might have. The next column lists various ways in which those needs could be met. In the third column are hypothetical community and family resources that might be available to you. The last two columns have hypothetical information in answer to the two questions: 1) "Can my needs adequately be met outside of a preschool experience?" and 2) "If no, what services or experiences do I expect the preschool to provide?"

A version of this table has been provided with blank spaces so that you might sketch in information relevant to your situation (Table 3.2). You might ask yourself and other family members the following two questions: 1) What are the most pressing needs of our family at this point? and 2) What person, place, or thing can best help us meet that need? After doing this, you probably will have a better idea of what steps are most important for you to take right now.

Table 3.1. Examples of different needs you may have and where and how those needs might be met

Parent needs	Ways in which needs can be met	Community and family resources for meeting needs	Can this need be met adequately outside of preschool?	If not, what services or experiences does the family expect preschool to provide?
Professional involvement with the education of the child so parents can relax	Preschool with competent and kind professionals to work with child on a regular basis	There are none. (In some locations, home intervention teams sponsored by local mental health centers offer services to handicapped children on a weekly basis, but these services are often limited to children under three years old.)	No	Preschool with a kind and competent staff
Reasonable cost of program	Preschool with a sliding fee scale or scholarships	Parents are able to find a program with a sliding fee scale	Yes	

Continued

Table 3.1—*Continued*

Parent needs	Ways in which needs can be met	Community and family resources for meeting needs	Can this need be met adequately outside of preschool?	If not, what services or experiences does the family expect preschool to provide?
	Preschool that is free, because it is subsidized by the local school system			
Convenience	Preschool that provides transportation	Family is able to be involved with a carpool	Yes	
	Preschool that arranges and encourages parent carpools			
	Preschool that is close enough to home so that transportation is not a problem			

Daycare services	Preschool that includes full-time daycare	Parents can find no after-school daycare program for child	No	Preschool with full-time daycare available
	Knowing a relative or a friend who can provide daycare for the remainder of the day after preschool hours			
	Having available another program that provides care for the remainder of the day after preschool hours			
Frequent contacts with the child's teachers	Preschool with opportunities for teacher conferences, visits to the classroom, and contact with teachers while dropping off and picking up children	None	No	Preschool with a staff able and willing to share information with parents frequently and in a give-and-take fashion
	Preschool with a staff interested in comments and feedback			

Continued

Table 3.1.—*Continued*

Parent needs	Ways in which needs can be met	Community and family resources for meeting needs	Can this need be met adequately outside of preschool?	If not, what services or experiences does the family expect preschool to provide?
	about the program from family members. Staff has time available to discuss various aspects of program and services with members of the family			
Counseling	Having available the services of professional counselor, i.e., social worker, psychiatrist, psychologist, or a skilled teacher who could offer individual or group therapy Having available parent support groups	Parents find that local parents' organizations (such as the Association for Retarded Citizens or the Association for Children with Learning Disabilities) have ongoing parent support groups	Yes	

Training	Having available workshops for family members on various topics, such as techniques for teaching and dealing with the child and parent rights and responsibilities	Parents find that local parents' organizations offer workshops	Yes
Opportunities to meet and talk with other parents	Preschool that provides opportunities for family members to talk together and to share information and feelings	Parents join local parents' organization	Yes
	Having opportunities to meet other parents of handicapped children through local parent organizations		

Table 3.2. Chart on parent needs for parents to complete

Parent needs	Ways in which needs can be met	Community and family resources for meeting needs	Can this need be met adequately outside of preschool?	If not, what services or experiences does the family expect preschool to provide?
Professional involvement with the education of the child so parents can relax	Preschool with competent and kind professionals to work with a child on a regular basis			
Reasonable cost of program	Preschool with a sliding fee scale or scholarships			
	Preschool that is free because it is subsidized by the local school system			
Convenience	Preschool that provides transportation			

Preschool that arranges and encourages parent carpools

Preschool that is close enough to home so that transportation is not a problem

Daycare services

Preschool that includes full-time daycare

Knowing a relative or a friend who can provide daycare for the remainder of the day after preschool hours

Having available another program that provides care for the remainder of the day after preschool hours

Continued

Table 3.2—*Continued*

Parent needs	Ways in which needs can be met	Community and family resources for meeting needs	Can this need be met adequately outside of preschool?	If not, what services or experiences does the family expect preschool to provide?
Frequent contacts with the child's teachers	Preschool with opportunities for teacher conferences, visits to the classroom, and contact with teachers while dropping off and picking up children			
Counseling	Having available the services of professional counselor, i.e., social worker, psychiatrist, psychologist, or a skilled teacher who could offer individual or group therapy			

Training	Having available parent workshops on various topics, such as dealing with the child and parent rights and responsibilities
Opportunities to meet and talk with other parents	Having opportunities to meet other parents of handicapped children through parents' organizations
	Community, neighborhood, church, and school contacts

WHAT KINDS OF PRESCHOOL PROGRAMS ARE AVAILABLE?

There are many ways in which preschool programs can be described or *typed.* Some of the different ways of typing programs are listed below:

1. The type of curriculum. *Curriculum* means the philosophy of education that guides the materials used and the way children are taught.
2. The type of agency that funds programs. Funding can come from private agencies like churches or the United Cerebral Palsy Foundation or from public agencies, such as local school systems or Headstart.
3. The location of the program. Programs can be *center based,* in which the child comes to a center for instruction, or *home based,* in which professionals come to the child's home to work with the child and parents.
4. The characteristics of the students for whom the program is primarily designed. Programs can be *specialized,* when

designed specifically for handicapped children, or *mainstreamed,* when designed primarily for nonhandicapped children.
5. The extent to which parents are involved in the program. Parent involvement can vary from programs that provide almost no activities for parents to programs that *require* parents to be highly involved in order for the child to be served.

In an attempt to answer the question "What type of preschool program is best for handicapped children?" educational researchers have examined and compared programs according to these major differences in types. A clear and simple answer pointing to the best type of program has not emerged. What is perhaps most clear is that programs of all types have been found to be successful. Much of what makes a program work involves a process unique to the individuals (directors, teachers, children, and parents) who are a part of the program. You cannot "bottle" the success of one preschool program and automatically transfer it to other programs. A highly successful program in one community can be duplicated by a different staff in a different community with excellent, mediocre, or poor results. Choosing a preschool is an important decision. It takes time and energy to seek out the program with the right combination of qualities to best suit your needs and those of your child.

There are no simple answers to the question, "What is the best type of preschool for handicapped children?" However, there is much information available that can help you in your consideration of the options in your community. The purpose of this section is to examine the concept of mainstreaming. Chapter 4 contains a description of what mainstreaming is, why there is currently so much emphasis on it, and how mainstreaming is defined by law. In Chapter 5, the complexities of the mainstreaming issue are detailed by providing a thorough description of the benefits and drawbacks of mainstreamed and specialized preschools, as experienced by parents of handicapped preschoolers.

Chapter 4

MAINSTREAMING: WHERE DID THE IDEA ORIGINATE AND WHAT DOES IT MEAN?

All parents face the questions of how much to protect their children, when to allow independence, and how much independence to allow. For parents of a handicapped child, these questions can be even more complicated.

A father of a sensory-impaired child expresses some of these complications:

I believe that parents should love their handicapped children as they are and work with everything they've got to help them reach their highest potential. But there is a fine line involved in doing this, almost a paradox. To love them as they are might tempt parents not to encourage them to achieve their highest potential, but rather to be content. On the other hand, placing emphasis on the child's reaching his or her highest potential could lead parents to dwell on what the child can't do. The result could be that it is harder to love them as they are.

Parents of handicapped children—particularly children with severe handicaps—cannot just relax and assume that one day their child will become an independently functioning adult. A double dilemma for parents can be created when they try to maximize their handicapped child's ability to function independently, but at the same time protect him or her from the threats of physical harm and emotional trauma brought on by the handicapping condition. The issues surrounding mainstreaming tie in closely with this dilemma.

One intent of mainstreaming is to improve the ability of handicapped persons to live as independently as possible by integrating them into regular school settings. However, this is only one side of the issue. One must also consider that this enhancement of independence through mainstreaming has not been proven; in fact, mainstreaming experiences may result in extremely positive outcomes for some handicapped children and negative outcomes for others. Of all of the issues surrounding the choice of a preschool, the issue of mainstreaming is the one that is probably most emotionally laden and confusing to parents.

It is understandable that parents may be confused about this idea. The term *mainstreaming* means many different things to many different people. Basically, "mainstreaming" can be defined as the education of handicapped children in classrooms with nonhandicapped children for at least a portion of the school day. The way mainstreaming is carried out varies from program to program and from community to community. The mother of a multiply handicapped preschooler sums up the ambivalence and confusion surrounding mainstreaming in her local school system with this statement: "Parents in this community are screaming! This is because the school officials are either shoving handicapped children into regular classes or trying to keep handicapped children all together in one place. To tell you the truth, I'm totally confused!" One way of understanding the idea of mainstreaming is by looking at the history of mainstreaming within the context of changing attitudes toward the treatment and education of handicapped persons.

THE HISTORY OF MAINSTREAMING

From the 1900's to the 1950's a common form of treatment for handicapped persons was placement in a residential institution and ultimate confinement there. Parents were generally not held responsible for the care, nurturing, or education of their handicapped child—in fact, frequently they were told to forget they had ever had the child. The prevalent thinking during this period is reflected in the following statement made by a physician:

Very frequently it will be the duty of the physician to convince the parents that the child would be better off in the state school than at home and to help with the procedures necessary to have the child admitted to the public institution. Even though the building may be old and crowded and the food scorned by Duncan Hines, the child will be among equals and will be able to compete with them, whereas in the home community the child will always be either overprotected or cruelly rejected by social contacts.[10]

The basic attitude of our society during this period was that handicapped people were hopeless cases to be isolated from society and cared for in a custodial fashion until they died. The families of handicapped children were provided with little help from community agencies. Children with significant handicaps were frequently excluded from school; mildly handicapped children who were in school were often considered laggards and misfits.

During this period, evidence slowly accumulated suggesting that the learning and development of institutionalized and mentally retarded children could be promoted through stimulation. This evidence led to a growing recognition and acceptance that, for this group, learning was possible.

Special classes for handicapped students began to spread rapidly during the 1950's and 1960's. It was felt that handicapped children could make progress if they could receive special instruction from special teachers in classes with small numbers of children. The philosophy of encouraging placement in special classes is reflected in the following quote from a special educator:

---

[10] Reed, S.C. 1963. *Counseling in Medical Genetics,* 2nd Ed. W.B. Saunders Co., Philadelphia.

Should it be judged that special class placement will probably be of most benefit to the child, then placement should be made without delay. Both the child and the parents should be told that the child is being transferred into the special class because the class is special. It will provide opportunities not available in the regular class, and the small class will allow the teacher to provide individual instruction of a type the child cannot get in a regular classroom. Teaching is based on a careful study of the child's learning characteristics, and the materials and programs are especially designed or selected to fit the characteristics. The entire program should be explained so the parents will understand what lies ahead for the child and so they can support the efforts of the teachers with the child. The special class should be described as an opportunity, not as a punishment for poor accomplishment or bad behavior.[11]

Classroom teachers typically were not expected to assume responsibility for teaching troublesome and problematic children in their regular classrooms. The development of special classes was welcomed by many parents and teachers alike. Parents at last were getting public support and help with their handicapped children through the increase of community-based programs and public school special education programs.

This basic approach, educating handicapped children separately from the regular classroom education of nonhandicapped children, continued until the late 1960's. At that time there was a rather abrupt shift in thinking and in attitudes toward what was the best way to educate handicapped children. Suddenly the same special classrooms that had been viewed as bringing promise and hope to handicapped children were seen as being stigmatizing and lacking in equality. Why such a change in thinking? There were several reasons why the practice of educating handicapped children in special classes was called into question.

Research on the outcomes of using special versus regular

---

[11] Kolstoe, O.P. 1970. *Teaching Educable Mentally Retarded Children*, p. 42. Holt, Rinehart & Winston, Inc., New York.

class education for handicapped children could not prove that special class placement improved the academic achievement of handicapped children. In fact, some of the research suggested that the effects of special class placement might be harmful to handicapped children by holding back their academic achievement or by stigmatizing them as being different. Perhaps the most damaging evidence against special classes was research proving that a larger than expected proportion of the students in special classes were from minority groups. Thus, special classes were viewed by some critics as a mechanism for minority and racial segregation.

The extent to which this information discredited special classes can best be understood if one thinks back to the social climate of our country during the 1960's. Radical changes were occurring then. Spearheaded by the civil rights movement, the right of minority groups to equal opportunities was the theme of that decade. Evidence that special classes did not improve the academic skills of handicapped children and that such classes might serve as a means of isolating handicapped persons and members of minority groups from the rest of society clearly offered grounds for questioning this educational practice.

At the same time that the superiority of special class placement over regular class placement for handicapped children was being questioned, the philosophy or idea of *normalization*[12] was transported from Europe and was making an impact on attitudes toward handicapped persons in this country. The idea of normalization basically means providing opportunities for handicapped people to have experiences as close as possible to the normal patterns of mainstreamed society. The assumption underlying this idea is that handicapped people will be more likely to develop normal characteristics and behaviors if they have experiences in normal settings. An important part of this idea is the recognition that society must also adapt to the needs of handicapped people. Captions for deaf persons on television, ramps and wide doorways in public buildings for people in wheelchairs, and parking spaces for handicapped persons are

---

[12] Wolfensberger, W. 1972. *The Principle of Normalization in Human Services.* National Institute on Mental Retardation, Toronto.

ways in which our society has become more accommodating. These accommodations allow handicapped people more opportunities to function in normalized settings.

An accompanying idea that has influenced attitudes toward the best educational practice for handicapped children is the notion of *dignity of risks*.[13] This term embodies the idea that allowing handicapped individuals to confront the challenges of life in the mainstream increases the likelihood that they eventually will learn how to deal with the real world. According to this principle, the idea of removing, protecting, and treating the handicapped children in an isolated setting only increases the likelihood that they will have to be "treated" for the rest of their lives. The ultimate goal for those who support normalization and dignity of risks is for handicapped persons to function independently and productively in a society that is willing to provide them with opportunities to do so.

Another factor contributing to the change in thinking about special classes is the recognition that interacting with nonhandicapped children can be a valuable learning experience for handicapped children. Research has suggested that being in structured play situations with nonhandicapped children can improve handicapped children's social and language skills.

A parent of an autistic child states why she believes her son has benefited from being in a classroom with nonhandicapped children:

*Bill is extremely withdrawn and would just as soon sit
in the corner and twittle a paper clip all day than
interact with others. The psychologist who evaluated
him encouraged my husband and me to enroll him in a
mainstreamed preschool. I'll be honest and admit that
we initially had grave doubts about Bill's chance of
success in that setting. We finally agreed to the
placement on a trial basis. The whole experience has
turned out to be very positive. The other children have a
knack for getting Bill involved. They ask him questions*

---

[13] Perske, R. 1972. The dignity of risk and the mentally retarded. *Mental Retardation,* 10:24–27.

*and they expect an answer. If he tries to ignore them,
they keep after him until he responds. In many ways, I
believe Bill has benefited from the other children as
much as from the teacher.*

These are factors that have led to the current practice of mainstreaming handicapped children. A culmination of historical influences leading to mainstreaming children with handicaps was the passage of federal and state legislation. This legislation requires the placement of handicapped children in the *least restrictive environment.*

HOW THE LEAST RESTRICTIVE ENVIRONMENT IS DEFINED BY LAW

The current thinking that the best educational placement for handicapped children should be in the least restrictive environment is *so strong* that this practice has been mandated by law. Public Law 94–142 states that handicapped children should be, to the maximum extent appropriate, educated with students who are nonhandicapped. Only when the nature or severity of the child's handicap is such that education in the regular school program cannot be successfully achieved, *even* with the aid of supplementary materials and specialists, can removal of the child from regular education be justified. In Chapter 6, the principle of the least restrictive environment is discussed in more detail.

An important part of this law is the guarantee that school systems should provide handicapped children with a wide range of placement options from which the least restrictive, but most appropriate, educational setting can be selected. To use the exact words of the law, the federal regulations specify that "each public agency shall ensure that a continuum of alternative placements is available to meet the needs of handicapped children for special education and related service."[14] The continuum of alternative placements should allow for choices in terms of the

---

[14] *Federal Register.* 1977. August 23, 1977, p. 42497. U.S. Government Printing Office, Washington, DC.

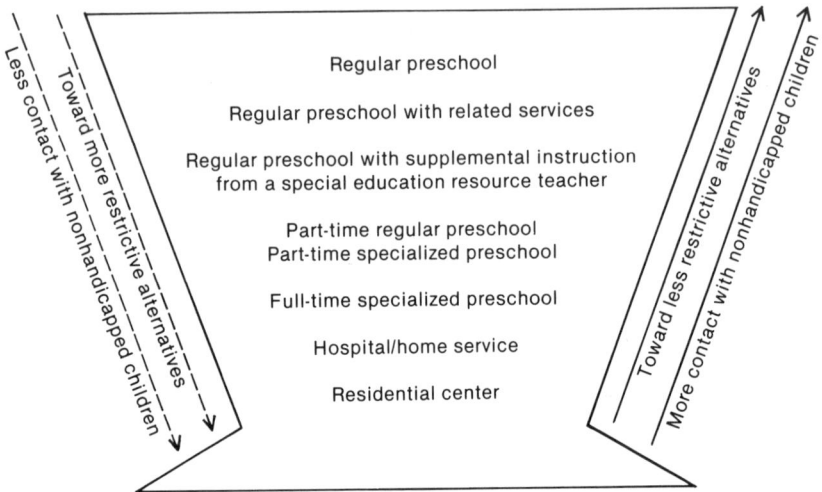

Figure 4.1. Placement alternatives.

closeness of programs to regular education. Figure 4.1 shows examples of the kinds of placement that should be available for you to consider. According to the law, each child's strengths and weaknesses should be individually considered with the important placement decision being made jointly by parents and professionals. In making that decision, parents should have a full range of options from which to choose.

There are two types of regular preschools that you may want to consider. The most frequent type is a regular preschool that has *traditional mainstreaming*. A preschool with traditional mainstreaming is primarily set up for nonhandicapped children but may be willing to serve a small number of handicapped youngsters. The teachers in such programs typically have backgrounds emphasizing early childhood education rather than special education. The other type of regular preschool is based on a *reverse mainstreaming* program. The reverse mainstreaming approach is devised from the outset to meet the needs of handicapped children but also enrolls children who are nonhandicapped. These programs either have handicapped children in the majority or serve approximately equal numbers of both groups. Because of the emphasis on working with the handicapped population, teachers usually are trained in special education. Reverse mainstreaming programs are relatively new and are not available in every community.

The principle of least restriction does *not* require that *all* handicapped children be educated in regular classes; rather it requires that handicapped children should be placed in regular classes when their individual needs can be appropriately met in that setting. Thus, handicapped children should be placed in special classes only when they cannot be educated successfully in regular classes.

The difference between the terms *mainstreaming* and *least restrictive placement* sometimes gets blurred. The important distinction is that mainstreaming refers to the placement of handicapped children in regular classes for at least a portion of the school day; whereas, the least restrictive placement may be any of the options that might be required to meet the special needs of the handicapped student, as listed in Figure 4.1. Some severely handicapped children may require the specialization available in special classes, special schools, hospitals, or institutions. If placed in such settings, a child could be in the least restrictive setting appropriate to his needs but still not be mainstreamed into a regular class.

REALITY AT THE PRESCHOOL LEVEL REGARDING PLACEMENT OPTIONS

Unfortunately, this full range of program types is not available in all communities, especially at the preschool level. In fact, whether or not your *preschool* handicapped child is guaranteed a free and appropriate education of any sort depends upon the state in which you reside. (See Table 6.2 in Chapter 6 for a listing of which states have laws ensuring the provision of preschool programs.) If you do not live in one of the states providing a legal guarantee of a preschool education, then chances are that placement options are even more limited. Even if you do live in a state in which preschool services for handicapped children are provided, this does not necessarily guarantee that your local school system provides a wide range of placement choices. In those states where preschool programs are provided for handicapped children, they are generally not available for nonhandicapped children below the age of five. This means that publicly supported mainstreaming opportunities are usually not available. With the exception of Headstart programs, which are mandated by law to include at least 10% handicapped children, most regular preschools are privately funded and are not required to serve handicapped children.

The relatively sudden condemnation of special classes and the accompanying enthusiasm over mainstreaming is viewed with caution and skepticism by some. For one thing, just as the research does not demonstrate the clearcut superiority of special classes, neither does it provide evidence that mainstreaming is always successful. There are successful programs of both types.

Some people question the assumption underlying mainstreaming—that placement in regular classes actually does increase the handicapped child's chances of leading a more independent life. They argue that developmental and academic delays set the handicapped child apart from nonhandicapped peers. By providing the child with special instruction (which may be provided best in special classes), they feel there is a better chance that delays will be remedied, so that in the long run the child will indeed function more independently in the real world. For example, some preschool blind children may need special mobility and orientation training, which is unavailable in most preschools for nonhandicapped children. By attending a specialized program, they may develop skills that will later help them to participate in a more normal environment. This perspective accepts the normalization principle, that a reasonable goal is for handicapped people to function as independently and as close to the norm as possible. Some parents and professionals are questioning the means of reaching that goal.

There are others who question the goal itself. They ask the basic question, "Is the quality of life of handicapped persons increased as they are shaped in the image of a so-called normal person?" They would argue that handicapped persons should be allowed to pursue their own definition of a quality life and to exercise their own choice on factors affecting their lifestyle. The mother of a profoundly retarded son expresses her disagreement with the normalization principle:

There are some parents who like the idea of normalization [Wolfensberger, 1972] because it is useful in glossing over the realities of certain differences. I sometimes think there are professionals who like it for the same reason. Rather than trying to create a normal environment for my son, I try to think of how the world must look from his point of view, and what kind of an environment would not only minimize his boredom and loneliness but enhance his sense of dominance. In an era of divergent lifestyles, it seems particularly ironic that we place such stress on normalization for the retarded.[15]

Placing some handicapped children in the least restrictive environment of the regular class might place increased demands on their parents and siblings to work with them at home to help them keep up with the pace of their nonhandicapped classmates. One father describes this situation:

I am beginning to question whether we made the right decision when we pushed to have Michael placed in a regular kindergarten. His developmental delays have resulted in his not being able to keep up with the progress of the other kids. Every night we work with him on writing his name, counting, and letters. It gets to be a real drag. My wife and I have dropped out of all civic activities. We miss those experiences; they're important to us and we feel badly about not doing our part in the community. It's ironic that Michael's placement in the least restrictive environment of the regular class in many ways requires us to live in a highly restrictive environment. I wonder how long we can keep it up.

These various perspectives make it clear that the mainstreaming issue is a complicated one. We believe that the least restrictive environment policy should be considered a guide in

---

[15] Boggs, E. 1978. Who is putting whose head in the sand or in the clouds as the case may be? In: A.P. Turnbull and H.R. Turnbull (eds.), *Parents Speak Out: Views from the other Side of the Two-way Mirror,* pp. 62–65. Charles E. Merrill Publishing Co., Columbus, OH.

making a placement decision, not a mandate for regular class-room placement. It is one of several factors to consider when selecting a preschool. The relative restrictiveness of an environment (how specialized it is) can only be judged in light of an individual child's needs. What might be the least restrictive environment for one child might be a highly restrictive environment for another child. The goal in making a placement decision is to achieve a balance between a child's needs for specialized instruction and the child's needs for interaction with nonhandicapped peers. It is difficult yet necessary to consider these needs in terms of both short- and long-range goals.

THERE IS MORE TO KNOW ABOUT MAINSTREAMING

Gaining an overview of the history of mainstreaming, understanding how the idea of the least restrictive environment is defined by law, and translating the principle into placement alternatives might be considered the first steps toward learning about this complicated issue. To get a better picture of how the choice of mainstreaming might affect your life and your child's life, it is helpful to look at what research on preschool mainstreaming has to tell us, especially research with parents who can provide an insider's perspective on this issue. The purpose of Chapter 5, which provides information based primarily on research with parents of handicapped children, is to help enlarge and enrich your understanding of mainstreaming at the preschool level.

Chapter 5

WHAT DO PARENTS SAY ABOUT PRESCHOOL MAINSTREAMING?

Much of the research on mainstreaming has focused on measures of outcome with regard to the child. Studies that examine the academic achievement of handicapped children in mainstreamed classes, the extent to which nonhandicapped children play with or like handicapped children in their class, and the types of language patterns and play activities in which handicapped and nonhandicapped children engage have provided us with valuable information about mainstreaming. However, studies of this type fail to provide a look at the broader picture of how such a preschool choice affects the family, and how this choice is made within the context of the neighborhood and community. The research that led to the development of this book focused on parents' perspectives on preschool mainstreaming. It was felt that a broader perspective on mainstreaming could be gained by asking parents of handicapped children who had recently made a preschool choice (whether they chose a mainstreamed or specialized program) why they made that particular choice, and how it affected them and their families.

Parents' perspectives on the pros and cons of mainstreamed and specialized preschools are presented in this chapter. This information is supplemented throughout with other relevant research findings. The picture that emerges should help to clarify your thinking about what type of program is best for you and for your child.

THE IMPACT OF PRESCHOOL MAINSTREAMING ON HANDICAPPED CHILDREN

Major Benefits

Many parents feel that one of the major benefits of preschool mainstreaming is the chance it provides the child for exposure to the real world. In a sense, these parents have accepted the *normalization principle* that early exposure to normal settings will increase the child's ability to live independently and to function in normal settings in the future.

The mother of a daughter with cerebral palsy, who was placed in a mainstreamed preschool, states:

You need to learn to deal with this world the way it's designed to run right now, which is toward the nonhandicapped. You cannot live in a sheltered environment, whether it be in your own home or in a private school for the handicapped, and then all of a sudden come of age and be thrown out into that world and never learn to deal with it. She [her daughter] has got to learn to deal with some of the cruelties the other children are going to come up with when they are with her. She's going to have to learn to take care of herself in situations where there is not someone there to protect her.

Another mother whose son is blind and attends a mainstreamed preschool offers her own thoughts: "If he's going to be successful as an adult, he's going to have to adjust to living in a sighted world. The world's not suddenly going to turn around and adjust to him as a blind individual."

The mother of a physically handicapped mainstreamed child in a public school kindergarten described why she thought mainstreaming was beneficial: "He's going to have to cope with all kinds of things. It's better that he starts when he's small. If we waited until he got older and then just put him out in the world, that would be kind of cruel."

Although there is no clearcut research data that can be considered proof that early mainstreaming experiences enhance later success in normal settings, some of the parents in our research study felt that they were able to see evidence that their handicapped children were making necessary adaptations to the real world, even during the first few weeks of being enrolled in mainstreamed preschools. Almost half (41%) of the parents whose children were in mainstreamed preschools described a period of adjustment that their child underwent. In one case, the handicapped child was actually abused by other children. This child was physically handicapped and had moved from a special program to a mainstreamed kindergarten classroom in the public school. His mother describes what happened to her son:

At first, some of the other kids would pick on him or beat him up or something, and he'd just let them pick on him. They called him names that really surprised me— "retarded," "cripple," or stuff like that, really bad names. But they quit doing that. He has finally learned to stand up for himself.

What is perhaps most interesting about the different adjustment problems described is that no parent thought of them as drawbacks to the child's program. In all cases, they were described as having been resolved over time. In some cases, the adjustment made was felt to be beneficial in preparing the handicapped child for the real world.

Some research evidence suggests that, from the teacher's perspective, success in regular public kindergarten classrooms depends more upon a child's ability to blend into the group and to work independently than it does upon a child's mastery of certain academic skills. The best preschool environment, of course, is the one that enhances basic skills, *in addition* to encouraging independence and successful interaction with groups of children. However, from the perspective of mothers, mainstreamed preschools seem to offer more opportunities for independence and blending into the group than do specialized preschools. The mother of a child with Down's syndrome who was enrolled in a mainstreamed preschool in the morning and a specialized preschool in the afternoon. She compares the two different types of preschools with regard to their providing the child with real-world exposure:

Wade is not a fragile child—he is not sickly, he is not allergic to this and that, not on 38 medications, and doesn't weigh 2% of what he should weigh. There are kids in the Developmental Center [the special preschool he attends in the afternoon] with all of those problems. You have to have a certain degree of willingness for risk-taking and self-exploration to learn, and that's what he gets at Treehouse [the mainstreamed preschool he attends in the morning]. They are so protective over there at the special preschool because they do have kids with all of those physical problems.

However, not all parents share this perspective on mainstreamed schools. A different point of view was provided by a mother of a physically handicapped child who chose a special placement: "He's pretty young to be the only one who's different. He needs to see a lot of people like himself doing a lot of productive things before he can forge out there and be 'Crusader Rabbit'."

This mother definitely believed in the importance of providing her son with experiences in the real world, but she felt he got enough of these opportunities in the neighborhood and community. What with attending an older brother's soccer games, playing with lots of children in the neighborhood, and participating in many church activities, her son did, indeed, have many real world experiences. These other activities provided the necessary balance to her son's specialized preschool. She comments on the benefits of both:

I'm a great believer in the idea that a special setting is great at school, but I also feel that Sam cannot be around handicapped kids all the time. So when he comes home, it's just total normalcy. All of his little buddies walk and run and do everything else.

Not all parents feel that the mere presence of other children in the neighborhood ensures that mainstreaming will happen in this setting. The mother of a preschool child with Down's syndrome described what she called the very subtle social ramifications associated with the choice of a mainstreamed versus a specialized preschool. She felt that the decision to send her son to the regular preschool sponsored by a nearby church, where most of the neighborhood children went, had been critical to his being included in the neighborhood play activities. He carpooled with neighboring children, meaning that lunchtime trade-offs were frequent (different mothers took turns having the children at their home for lunch so the other mothers could extend their mornings off). By being on the same schedule as the other children, his inclusion in the group was automatic. The mother noticed that among her older daughter's neighborhood friends, those children who attended schools outside of the neighborhood (e.g., private schools) were soon excluded from the group. Simply because their schedules were different, and because they got home at different times by different means, it was harder for them to be part of the neighborhood network of children. From this mother's perspective, attending a school outside of the neighborhood affects a child's social life, whether the child is handicapped or not.

Each neighborhood and community offers unique opportunities for the handicapped child to experience real world exposure. You will want to think carefully about your own situation and how your choice of a preschool will affect and will complement such neighborhood and community activities in your child's life.

Learning Opportunities for Handicapped Children Many parents feel that a major benefit of a mainstreamed preschool is that it provides opportunities for their handicapped child to learn from and to imitate children who are more advanced. The mother of a preschooler with Down's syndrome describes why she thinks this is a benefit of her daughter's mainstreamed preschool:

I feel that at this point in Kay's life she needs to be with normal children because she does copy a lot—she's very good at mimicking. If she were around children like herself all the time, children who sit around and repeat and repeat and repeat the same phrase, there's the possibility that she would copy that and not learn as much.

A father of a mobility-impaired child in a wheelchair also values the opportunity for his son to learn from nonhandicapped classmates:

When I was a kid, playing ball was what I lived for. To me, that's part of what it means to be a boy. One of my hardest adjustments has been coming to grips with the fact that Ben can never participate in sports the way that I always did. But I have been pleasantly surprised with what Ben has learned on the playground with the other little guys in his kindergarten class. He can play tetherball with the best of them. They also are beginning to shoot basketball in a lowered goal. He sees the others doing it, and it motivates him to get out there and participate. It's helped me realize that Ben can enjoy sports, too.

In contrast, the mother of a young boy with spina bifida likes the opportunities her son has for competing on an equal basis with other handicapped children at a special school for children with cerebral palsy. She explains:

Everybody there is in the same boat. They play basketball, they go swimming once a week, they do all of these things that he wouldn't be able to do at a regular school. And he does these things with children who are like him—who are operating with the same limitations.

Research supports parents' perceptions that being in preschools with nonhandicapped children can enhance the learning of handicapped children. Carefully done studies in mainstreamed preschools have shown that nonhandicapped children are able to adjust their language to handicapped children in a way that encourages communication and the development of language skills. Such adjustment is done in much the same way that parents and older siblings adjust their language to younger children. Apparently, not only do nonhandicapped children provide models for more complex speech for the handicapped children to imitate, but they also are responsive listeners.

Benefits for Nonhandicapped Children Just as handicapped children can benefit from their interactions with nonhandicapped children, the situation can also work in reverse. We conducted a survey with parents of both handicapped and nonhandicapped children on the benefits and drawbacks of mainstreaming in kindergarten classes. Both groups of parents indicated that a major benefit of mainstreaming is the opportunity for nonhandicapped children to develop sensitivity about individual differences. A parent of a nonhandicapped child reports:

Sarah is having a wonderful experience as a result of a friendship she has developed with Kim, a classmate who is mentally retarded. Until this year, Sarah had never had a chance to get to know a person with a handicap. She is eager to finish her own work so she can help Kim. As she explains tasks to Kim, she ends up with a clearer understanding herself. She also is very sensitive to any slights toward Kim on the playground. Sarah has learned invaluable lessons about humaneness—lessons that never could have been learned from a book or from any advice I might have given her. We saw Kim's parents at a soccer game last Saturday. They told me how thankful they are that Sarah and Kim are friends, because Kim has learned a lot from Sarah. I told them that the friendship has definitely had reciprocal benefits. Kim has been Sarah's "teacher," just as Sarah has been Kim's.

The potential benefit of mainstreaming for society as a whole was addressed in a recent publication:

I think we always need to keep in mind that it's not just the children with special needs who are benefiting from this—the other children benefit just as much. If we could rear a generation of people who would not turn their heads when they meet somebody on the street who looks a little different from themselves or who walks in a particular kind of gait, I think it would be a great humanitarian step ahead. I would like to see mainstreaming really be thought about in terms of developing an attitude within the teachers, and thereby within the children, of a general acceptance of people who have special needs.[16]

In contrast to the satisfaction with the stimulating peer group felt by parents whose children were mainstreamed, some parents whose children were in specialized preschools were dissatisfied with their child's peer group. This was particularly true in certain programs, such as developmental centers, in which children with many different types of handicaps were served. Some parents felt that this situation made it impossible for teachers and specialists to have time for their own children. The concern did not seem to be restricted to one particular handicap group. Some parents of physically handicapped children in these settings were concerned that their children's intellectual abilities were not being challenged because of the presence of mentally retarded children. Some parents of mentally retarded children felt that their children's needs for normalizing experiences and active exploration of the environment were inhibited by the presence of a large number of immobile and fragile children with physical handicaps. Other parents felt that important activities, such as creative and dramatic play, were limited because of the low level of functioning of the group as a whole.

Research indicates that the optimal situation for handicapped children is to be with children at similar levels of development as well as with children who are more advanced. When children are equals in a situation, the responsibility of initiating and maintaining play or conversation rests on both children. Each child must work in the situation; each child grows as a result. Being with more advanced children is also important. The advanced child often takes on a tutorial, teacher-like role in the situation, thus modeling more complicated behavior and teaching as well.

Research also suggests that the characteristics of the handicapped child should be considered in the choice of mainstreaming. The more severe the handicap, the less able the child will

---

[16] Stixrud, W.R. (ed.). 1982. *Plain Talk about Early Education and Development.* Center for Early Education and Development, University of Minnesota, Minneapolis.

be able to benefit from being with nonhandicapped children. Children who are extremely active, rejecting or aggressive, or who are strongly avoided by peers often have difficulty in mainstreamed situations. Lyn Isbell's[17] hindsight perspective on her son's preschool experience illustrates that generalizations about who can and who cannot be mainstreamed should be made cautiously:

When my son started school I "knew" he had to go into a special program for severely retarded people. I "knew" this when I put him into a preschool when he was three. I knew wrong. Or at least I think I knew wrong after ten years of hindsight. The program I put him into (the only one available, by the way) served much older children, too, and some of them had severe behavior problems. My son is still trying to unlearn some of the rotten behavior he learned in that program. Perhaps he would have done better in a program with children who were younger, but nonhandicapped.

Another factor to consider is the role of the teacher in determining the extent to which the mainstreaming situation is a successful one. Research has shown that just because handicapped and nonhandicapped preschoolers are in the same classroom does not necessarily mean that they will play together. Teachers play a crucial role in organizing play, assigning roles based upon the child's ability to succeed, and then gradually withdrawing to let the children carry on independently. Other teacher qualities that have been identified as being important to the success of mainstreamed classrooms include:

1. Ability and willingness to model acceptance and support of individual differences
2. Ability to respond effectively to questions about a child's handicap
3. General knowledge of normal development, of handicapping conditions, and of specialized curriculum

---

[17] Isbell, L. 1983. Your child, education, the law, and how to stand up to it all. In: T. Dougan, L. Isbell, and P. Vyas (eds.), *We Have Been There: A Guidebook for Parents of People with Mental Retardation*. Abingdon Press, Nashville, TN.

4. Knowledge of resource personnel, such as specialists and consultants, and ability to use them.

The important point is that the benefits of mainstreaming identified by parents may not occur automatically. Research shows that many factors contribute to a successful mainstreaming experience. If you decide to consider a mainstreamed preschool for your child, it is important to look closely at what goes on within various mainstreamed preschools.

Major Drawbacks

Parents seem to feel that the major drawbacks to preschool mainstreaming for their children are instructional ones. Teachers in mainstreamed preschools are less likely than teachers in specialized preschools to be trained to deal with handicapped children. Teachers lacking training in special education may have less confidence in their ability to teach handicapped children. Research has shown that teachers' lack of confidence in their ability to teach handicapped children is associated with negative attitudes toward mainstreaming. An additional research finding that is relevant to this issue is that there are few actual differences between the teaching techniques used by regular teachers and those used by specialized teachers. The major difference between regular and special classes is in class size. Regular class teachers teach in large groups, whereas special class teachers provide more individual instruction. It may be the teacher's level of confidence rather than the level of training that is the important factor in a teacher's acceptance of handicapped children. The role of the teacher as the most important figure in determining the success of your child's school experience is almost beyond question. Therefore, when you are considering different preschools, the teachers' willingness to accept handicapped children and their confidence that they can do a good job with your child are extremely important criteria for you to consider.

Special services, such as speech and physical therapy, are less likely to be provided in mainstreamed programs than they are in specialized programs—particularly when the program is sponsored by an agency (e.g., churches) other than the public schools. If these services are crucial for your child's progress, then this is an important factor to consider. If these services are available elsewhere in the community, you may want to consider the additional cost and effort that will be required on your part to arrange for the needed services.

Mainstreamed preschools frequently have more children per teacher than special preschools. As a result, some parents believe that the lack of individualized instruction is a drawback of preschool mainstreaming. A mother of a blind child comments:

At first I was very enthusiastic about mainstreaming. I very much wanted my child to attend our church-sponsored preschool. Unfortunately, it just didn't work out for Sandra. The teacher was very uptight about having Sandra in class. Because she didn't want to do the wrong thing, she essentially ended up ignoring Sandra. As long as Sandra would occupy herself listening to records or playing with clay or just fiddling for a long period of time, the teacher would devote her attention to the other children. I talked with the teacher about my concerns and she admitted to me that she had really rather not have Sandra. The whole situation was disappointing, but I knew removing her from class was the best thing. It was clear that Sandra's special needs were not being met.

What you must consider is your own child's needs for individual instruction. Is this factor crucial to your child's skill development in certain areas? Are aides or volunteers available in mainstreamed preschools who might be able to give your child the extra attention that you think is needed?

It should be emphasized that these drawbacks to mainstreaming do not necessarily exist in all mainstreamed settings. It is important that you consider and evaluate these factors as you look at preschools and think about your child's needs.

IMPACT OF PRESCHOOL MAINSTREAMING ON PARENTS

Searching for a Preschool Program

Our research with parents makes it clear that the choice of mainstreaming has an impact on parents as well as on their handicapped child. Parents who feel that a mainstreamed program may be appropriate for their handicapped child often find that locating regular preschools willing to accept handicapped children is a major stumbling block. Publicly supported mainstreamed preschools, with the exception of Headstart programs and some public schools, are limited. They simply do not exist in most communities. Even if you live in one of the states in which preschool services are guaranteed for handicapped children, which should ensure your child a wide range of placement choices, you probably will not find a publicly supported, mainstreamed preschool. Frequently states meet the legal requirements to serve handicapped preschool children by providing financial support to existing developmental centers that enroll exclusively handicapped children. School officials may even put pressure on parents to place their handicapped children at these centers because of this funding arrangement. School officials may not know about or may not recommend mainstreamed preschool programs in the community receptive to handicapped children. If you feel strongly that a developmental center does not provide your child with an appropriate education in the least restrictive environment then you have the right (if you live in a state guaranteeing preschool services) to ask the school system to arrange for placement of your child in another setting, such as a private preschool program.

Finding regular preschool programs willing to accept handicapped children will frequently be left up to you—particularly if you live in a state that is not required or does not choose to serve preschool handicapped children. This search may entail hours of personal and sometimes painful investigation. One mother describes her own search for a regular preschool:

I won't ever forget when the infant program Christy had been in suggested that I find a regular preschool for her, and I started calling around. I called one preschool that was near us at the Methodist church. The director was wonderful. She said that they wanted to see Christy and that she would talk to the teacher of four-year-olds about taking Christy. And then she called me back up and said that the teacher refused to see Christy and that

*she couldn't have a child with Down's syndrome. She
was labeling Christy. And I sat down and I just cried,
and thought, "She won't even give my child a chance." It
wouldn't hurt if she had seen Christy and said, "I don't
think it's going to work out," because I wasn't sure it
was going to work out. It was a test situation. I didn't
know if Christy could cope with it. But they could have
given her a chance to try.*

Unfortunately, few communities have a clearinghouse or resource center where information on regular preschools can be found. Other parents of handicapped children in your community who have recently been through the preschool decision-making process are probably the best resource for locating appropriate regular preschools.

Additional Responsibilities for Parents

Mainstreaming may place additional responsibilities on parents in terms of their needing to supplement missing services. One mother makes this comment:

*After driving Ed ten miles each way to the preschool
where he was being mainstreamed, we still had to take
him to three additional therapists several times each
week. He was spending so much time in the car that we
were unable to work with him on his toilet training.*

It may be harder for parents to relax, even knowing that competent professionals are working with their child, if their child is in a mainstreamed preschool with teachers who nevertheless are not used to teaching handicapped children. The mother of a physically handicapped child in a Headstart program (mainstreamed) described the duties this situation required of her. She recalls:

*I had to sit down and tell Andrea's teacher everything. I
told him about the different types of exercises that the
therapist wanted Andrea to have in school, how to put
braces on, how to take her braces off—everything. I
really had to lay it on the line.*

In this situation the mother did not mind showing her child's teacher how to manage her child's braces and exercises; what the mother *did* mind was that the teacher never followed through on any of the exercises unless the mother was present.

Association with Children and Their Parents

Some parents we interviewed felt that seeing their child with other handicapped children made them feel better about their own child's handicapping condition. The mother of a physically handicapped child describes how she felt when she first visited her son's specialized preschool: "Seeing the other kids' conditions—more severe than my son's—helped me adjust. I was not aware that so many children were handicapped before then. I realized that we were not the only ones with a handicapped child."

Other parents had negative reactions to seeing their children in a group of handicapped children. The mother of a visually impaired preschooler describes how she felt the first time she visited the specialized program in her community:

When I saw the kids over there, how badly handicapped they were, I said, "My child doesn't belong here." There were very severely mentally retarded children, and I could not help but wonder, "Is this the place for Dan?" I couldn't help but be concerned.

Ultimately this mother decided that the specialized preschool was the best choice for her son and one year later was very pleased with her decision, in spite of her initial reactions to his peer group.

Parents also experienced emotional reactions to seeing their handicapped child among nonhandicapped children. Several parents felt as if their handicapped child might be better equipped or better able to benefit from the real world exposure offered in mainstreamed preschools than the parents themselves would be. This is because the handicapped child either would not notice the rejection or teasing that might come his way or could adjust to it. The mother of a mentally retarded child describes her reactions to visiting a regular preschool when trying to decide upon a preschool for her daughter: "I was afraid children might be cruel to her because she is so different. They might laugh at her or pick at her. It might not have an effect on her, but it would hurt me." This mother eventually settled on a specialized preschool.

Some parents felt that seeing their child among normally developing peers caused them additional anguish over their own child's limitations. The mother of a child with cerebral palsy who attended a mainstreamed preschool describes how certain scenes on the playground would cause her to feel sad about her daughter's physical limitations:

When I pick up Sue, the children are always out on the playground. Sometimes Sue and some other kids will be playing in the sandbox, and then suddenly the action will move to another part of the playground, and Sue will be left in the sandbox all alone. When I come up she doesn't seem unhappy to be alone—sometimes I don't think she even notices. But I just want to grab her up and be her legs and run with her after the other children. I don't know if I'll ever get over that feeling!

Even though this mother wondered if she would ever get used to seeing her daughter left behind by other children, research indicates that parents adjust to these mainstreaming incidents over time. One mother, whose Down's syndrome daughter attended a mainstreamed preschool, felt that her own sadness over seeing her daughter in the midst of normally developing children had gradually disappeared. She reported that her husband, on the other hand, still had pangs of grief when he saw their daughter on the playground with the other children on the occasional days that he picked her up from school. She felt that she had gotten over her sadness through daily exposure to the situation, whereas her husband had not had enough exposure to adjust to the differences.

Another consequence of choosing a mainstreamed or a specialized preschool for your child is that the other parents associated with the preschool will be predominately parents of nonhandicapped children or predominately parents of handicapped children. A few mothers that we interviewed felt that being around parents of normally developing children broadened their experiences and understanding of other people, especially if the mother had only a handicapped child. Sometimes parents of handicapped children find themselves overly drawn into the handicapped world. One mother of a physically handicapped, mainstreamed child describes the gain in perspective she experienced in the mainstreamed preschool:

I'm glad that I got to meet new people, because I find that a lot of times I am only exposed to parents of handicapped children or to the professionals who work in the field. I don't really get to talk to other parents about their children in general. I started to appreciate that they have problems too.

This mother further related that, being in the minority, she had to work very hard at presenting her handicapped child's special needs and her own concerns to the other parents. She felt that, by being a member of the Parent Advisory Board of the preschool, she could ensure that her daughter's needs for things like adaptive play equipment were clearly identified and acted upon. Without her active involvement, she felt that the placement would have been much less successful.

Some mothers report occasional feelings of not being accepted by other parents in mainstreamed settings because of their child's handicap. A mother, whose daughter with cerebral palsy attended a mainstreamed preschool, explains how she felt at the beginning of the school year:

When I first started taking Stephanie to Cloverleaf Preschool, it was a little unusual because I felt like most of the parents didn't speak to me. It was like either they were afraid to get involved in a conversation with me or they really didn't know how to deal with the situation.

In most cases, parents felt as if the parents of nonhandicapped children started feeling more relaxed with them as time went on. One mother recounted an incident that occurred in the observation room of her son's mainstreamed preschool. The anecdote illustrates how a lively sense of humor can help put parents of nonhandicapped children at ease: "What is really comical is when you meet people in the observation room, and they say, 'Mine is the little girl with the blue ribbon, which one is yours?' Then I say, 'Well, mine is the one with the skull cap on and the two braces—how can you miss him?' "

A factor that seems to aid parent-to-parent interaction in mainstreamed preschools is the extent to which the handicapped child plays with other children or becomes friends with them. The mother who felt that other parents did not speak to her at the beginning of the year goes on to describe how and why that situation changed: "The funny thing is that Stephanie brought them around. At the end of the year every one of the parents came up to me and wanted to tell me how much they and their children enjoyed getting to know Stephanie."

Some research on parent-to-parent interaction in mainstreamed settings verifies that parents of handicapped children in those settings may feel somewhat isolated. The research suggested that parents are likely to develop closer relationships with the parents of their children's friends and also with neighbors. For handicapped children, making friends may be more problematic. Factors other than proximity of the preschool to home may take the handicapped child away from the neighborhood preschool.

In contrast, many parents whose children attended specialized preschools describe their associations with other parents as being a source both of emotional support and of important information. A father expresses this point of view as follows:

*Until Kathy was enrolled in a special preschool, I had
never known another father of a handicapped youngster.
I am not really the kind of person who seeks out
professional counseling, but I realized that I had a lot of
hurt inside and tremendous worry over the financial
implications of Kathy's numerous surgeries and therapy.
I saw a notice on the preschool announcement board
about a meeting just for fathers. My first reaction was to
avoid it, but I kept thinking that maybe it would help
me work some things out. I ended up going and it
turned out to be one of the most positive experiences I
have ever had. More than anything, I found out that my
concerns are no different from those of many other*

fathers. We ended up having monthly meetings. At one of them, a lawyer explained tax regulations pertaining to medical expenses and estate planning. It was the type of information I greatly needed.

Again, the major issue to consider is your own situation. Are you looking for chances to meet with and talk to other parents of handicapped children? Are opportunities for such contact available elsewhere in the community?

MAKING A DECISION ABOUT MAINSTREAMING

In summing up what parents say about the issue of mainstreaming, it is clear that the choice is based upon a delicate balancing of needs and priorities and a careful consideration of neighborhood, family, and community factors. On the positive side, most of the parents we interviewed felt that they had worked out a satisfactory preschool arrangement for their child and for their family. For one family, this meant enrolling their handicapped child in two different preschool programs—a mainstreamed program in the morning and a specialized program in the afternoon. For other families, the *reverse mainstreamed preschool,* serving equal numbers of handicapped and nonhandicapped children, provided the best of both worlds. One mother describes the benefits of this choice in these words:

At school, the ratio of teachers to children was such that they could take care of my daughter's special needs; at the same time, there would be enough normal children around so she would be exposed to them also. She was still in diapers, and that's very hard to handle in a public school situation. But it was a place where other people were wearing diapers, too, where she didn't have to say "I'm the only one"—that is what we wanted.

Asking the simple question "Which is best—mainstreamed or specialized preschools?" can lead to a few useful conclusions. Careful consideration of what goes on *within* the preschool program, and how this interaction meets the needs of the child and of the family, is the key to deciding upon the best preschool for your child.

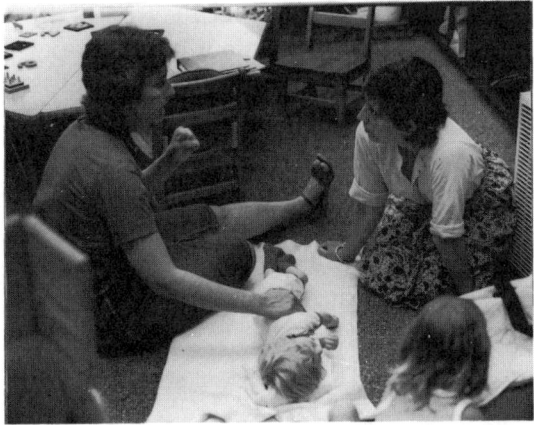

HOW DO YOU GATHER INFORMATION AND SELECT THE MOST APPROPRIATE PRESCHOOL PROGRAM FOR YOUR CHILD?

The major focus of this book has been on helping you to think about your child and family and about what kinds of things you might want from a preschool experience. This might be considered the first step in the decision-making process. The next step in the process is gathering information about the preschools available in your community. The final step is for you to select the preschool program that you feel is closest to what you ideally want. The purpose of this section is to provide facts and suggestions to help you gather information and select a program.

Chapter 6

WHAT ARE YOUR CHILD'S LEGAL RIGHTS AND YOUR LEGAL RIGHTS AND RESPONSIBILITIES?

It is the purpose of this Act to assure that all handicapped children have available to them . . . a free, appropriate public education which emphasizes special education and related services designed to meet their unique needs, to assure that the rights of handicapped children and their parents or guardians are protected, to assist States and localities to provide for the education of all handicapped children, and to assess and assure the effectiveness of efforts to educate handicapped children (Section 601c, Public Law 94–142).

Section 601c is taken from a federal law that has dramatically improved the chances that your child will receive an appropriate education from the public school system. One of the parts of the law that is most revolutionary is that parents have certain legal rights and responsibilities in connection with the planning of the handicapped child's educational program. The law is long and complex; however, your understanding of it is a critical factor in ensuring that your child receives the education to which he or she is entitled. As the father of a severely handicapped child states: "In order to ensure that my child has the best possible life, I have got to know what his rights are and what my rights are." Some of the questions frequently asked by parents and the answers to those questions are included below.

WHY WERE THESE LAWS ENACTED FOR HANDICAPPED CHILDREN WHEN THERE ARE NO SIMILAR LAWS FOR CHILDREN WHO ARE NOT HANDICAPPED?

A Congressional study carried out before the passage of P.L. (Public Law) 94–142 showed that more than half of the handicapped children in the United States were not receiving an appropriate education. In many cases handicapped children were not provided with any sort of public school education and few chances existed for preschool education. As Lynn Isbell[18] puts it: "The contrast between the education provided for the handicapped child in a family and that provided for his nonhandicapped brothers and sisters just got to be more than many parents could stand." She goes on to recount what it was like for parents before federal and state laws were passed guaranteeing education for handicapped children:

[Parents spent] years running their own day care centers, begging for about-to-be-torn-down buildings from cities and counties, [holding] raffles and cake sales, [fighting] ever higher tuition costs, and [having] no transportation except car pools. This was the educational system for handicapped children of school age. Parents went through all of the hardships above, and more, and all for programs that were constantly running on a shoestring, about to go under, about to be evicted and quite often not much more than a kind of group babysitting anyway. For many years this was considered good enough for children who were demonstrating daily that they did have the ability to learn.

---

[18] Isbell, L. 1983. Your child, education, the law, and how to stand up to it all. In: T. Dougan, L. Isbell, and P. Vyas (eds.), *We Have Been There: A Guidebook for Parents of People with Mental Retardation.* Abingdon Press, Nashville, TN.

WHAT ARE THE SOURCES OF LAW ON EDUCATING HANDICAPPED CHILDREN?

The law on the education of handicapped children is made at federal, state, and local levels. At the federal level, there is Public Law 94–142, the *Education for All Handicapped Children Act.* P.L. 94–142 was passed by Congress in November, 1975. The regulations for implementation were published in the *Federal Register* of August 23, 1977. A copy of this register can be requested from the United States Government Printing Office in Washington, D.C.

The second source of law is state legislation. Every state except New Mexico has legislation on educating handicapped children. At the state level, the executive agency in the state with responsibility for education (this agency goes by various names, including the Department of Education and the Department of Public Instruction) issues regulations for carrying out state legislation. Information on how to get copies of this legislation and the regulations involved can be obtained from the Department of Education in each state.

The Board of Education at the local level also makes decisions about how to carry out federal and state law. Information on local policy and regulations can be obtained from the Director of Special Education in each school system.

WHAT IS THE LEGAL DEFINITION OF "HANDICAPPED CHILDREN"?

According to P.L. 94–142, *handicapped children* means those children evaluated as being mentally retarded, hard of hearing, deaf, speech impaired, visually handicapped, seriously emotionally disturbed, orthopedically impaired, other health impaired, or as having specific learning disabilities, and who, because of those impairments, need special education and related services. A definition of each of these handicaps is included in Table 6.1.

Generally, the definitions of "handicapped" in state legislation are similar to those included in P.L. 94–142. In some states, the legislation refers to "children with special needs" or "exceptional children" and covers the additional classification of gifted and talented.

Table 6.1. Legal definitions of handicapped children

The term *handicapped children* means those children evaluated as being mentally retarded, hard of hearing, deaf, speech impaired, visually handicapped, seriously emotionally disturbed, orthopedically impaired, other health impaired, deaf-blind, multiply handicapped, or as having specific learning disabilities, who because of those impairments need special education and related services.

The terms used in this definition are defined as follows:

1) *Deaf* means a hearing impairment that is so severe that the child is impaired in processing linguistic information through hearing, with or without amplification, which adversely affects educational performance.

2) *Deaf-blind* means concomitant hearing and visual impairments, the combination of which causes such severe communication and other developmental and educational problems that they cannot be accommodated in special education programs solely for deaf or blind children.

3) *Hard of hearing* means a hearing impairment, whether permanent or fluctuating, that adversely affects a child's educational performance but that is not included under the definition of "deaf" in this section.

4) *Mentally retarded* means significantly subaverage general intellectual functioning existing concurrently with deficits in adaptive behavior and manifested during the developmental period, which adversely affects a child's educational performance.

5) *Multiply handicapped* means concomitant impairments (such as mentally retarded-blind, mentally retarded-orthopedically impaired), the combination of which causes such severe educational problems that they cannot be accommodated in special programs solely for one of the impairments. The term does not include deaf-blind children.

6) *Orthopedically impaired* means a severe orthopedic impairment that adversely affects a child's educational performance. The term includes impairments caused by congenital anomaly (e.g., clubfoot, absence of some member), impairments caused by disease (e.g., poliomyelitis, bone tuberculosis), and impairments from other causes (e.g., cerebral palsy, amputations, and fractures or burns that cause contractures).

7) *Other health impaired* means
   i) having an autistic condition that is manifested by severe communication and other developmental and educational problems; or
   ii) having limited strength, vitality or alertness, because of

chronic or acute health problems, such as a heart condition, tuberculosis, rheumatic fever, nephritis, asthma, sickle cell anemia, hemophilia, epilepsy, lead poisoning, leukemia, or diabetes, which adversely affects a child's educational performance.

8) *Seriously emotionally disturbed* is defined as follows:
 i) The term means a condition exhibiting one or more of the following characteristics over a long period of time and to a marked degree, which adversely affects educational performance:
  A) An inability to learn that cannot be explained by intellectual, sensory, or health factors
  B) An inability to build or maintain satisfactory interpersonal relationships with peers and teachers
  C) Inappropriate types of behavior or feelings under normal circumstances
  D) A general pervasive mood of unhappiness or depression
  E) A tendency to develop physical symptoms of fears associated with personal or school problems.
 ii) The term includes children who are schizophrenic. The term does not include children who are socially maladjusted, unless it is determined that they are seriously emotionally disturbed.

9) *Specific learning disability* means a disorder in one or more of the basic psychological processes involved in understanding or in using language, spoken or written, which may manifest itself in an imperfect ability to listen, think, speak, read, write, spell, or to do mathematical calculations. The term includes such conditions as perceptual handicaps, brain injury, minimal brain dysfunction, dyslexia, and developmental aphasia. The term does not include children who have learning problems that are primarily the result of visual, hearing, or motor handicaps, of mental retardation, or of environmental, cultural, or economic disadvantage.

10) *Speech impaired* means a communication disorder, such as stuttering, impaired articulation, a language impairment, or a voice impairment, which adversely affects a child's educational performance.

11) *Visually handicapped* means a visual impairment that, even with correction, adversely affects a child's educational performance. The term includes both partially seeing and blind children.

From: *Federal Register.* 1977. pp. 42478–42479; 1981, pp. 3865–3866. (The definitional change of autism from the category of *seriously emotionally disturbed* to *other health impaired* is reported in the 1977 *Federal Register.*)

WHAT AGES OF HANDICAPPED CHILDREN
ARE COVERED BY P.L. 94–142 AND BY STATE LAW?

There is no simple answer to this question. P.L. 94–142 requires states to have provided free appropriate educational opportunities to all handicapped children in the age range of 3 to 18 by September 1, 1978, and to all handicapped children in the age range of 3 to 21 by September 1, 1980. There are, however, legal exceptions to these requirements for the age ranges of 3–5 and 18–21. As applied to the preschool population, these exceptions are as follows:

1. States do not have to provide educational programs to preschool handicapped children if they do not provide such opportunities to preschool nonhandicapped children.

2. If a state does provide nonhandicapped children with preschool programs, they must serve at least a proportionate number of handicapped children of the same age.

3. The state may not discriminate against preschool handicapped children by requiring that some be included in programs and others be excluded; rather, requirements to provide an educational program must apply to all children with the same handicap and of the same age.

Based on information gathered in 1982, a summary of mandated and permissive age ranges served by each state is included in Table 6.2. States who have laws on serving preschool children must develop programs that comply with federal and state regulations for educating handicapped children. These regulations are discussed later in the chapter.

You will need to locate your state in Table 6.2 to find out if your state has either mandated or permissive preschool programs. If your state is mandated to serve handicapped children in the preschool age range, you have a legal guarantee of services. Permissive services mean that the state is not *required* to provide preschool services, but does have the *option* to do so. Thus, you may find that services are, indeed, available. States with permissive services still must comply with the legal requirements discussed in this chapter. The age at which handicapped children are ensured a free appropriate education depends upon the state in which the child resides, and these

Table 6.2. Mandated and permissive legislation chart

State	Mandated	Permissive
Alabama	6–21	3–5
Alaska	3–19	0–21 (except GT[a])
Arizona	5–21	—
Arkansas	6–21	0–5
California	3–21 Substantially handicapped	
	4.9–21 Others	0–3
Colorado	5–21	Below age 5
Connecticut	5–21	0–5
Delaware[b]	4–20 (EMH, SEM, LD, SI)	
	3–20 (TMH, PI, A)	
	0–20 (HI, VI, DB)	0–4 Categories not mandated
D.C.	4–21	—
Florida	5–18	0–4
Georgia	5–18	0–21
Hawaii	3–20	—
Idaho	7–16	5–21
Illinois	3–21	0–2
Indiana	6–18	3–5
Iowa	0–21	21–24
Kansas	Kdg. until 21	0–21
Kentucky	5–17	0–4, 18–21
Louisiana	3–21	0–21
Maine	5–20	—
Maryland	0–21	—
Massachusetts	3–21	0–21
Michigan	0–25	—
Minnesota	4–21	0–4
Mississippi	6–20	0–5

Continued

[a] Abbreviations used in this table are: A, autistic; AI, aural impairment; DB, deaf/blind; EMH, educable mentally handicapped; GT, gifted/talented; HH, hearing handicapped; HI, hearing impairment; LD, learning disability; MR, mentally retarded; PI, physical impairment; SEM, social or emotional maladjustment; SI, speech impairment; TMH, trainable mentally handicapped; VI, visual impairment.

[b] As of 7/82, autistic will be served down to birth.

Table 6.2—*Continued*

State	Mandated	Permissive
Missouri	5–21	3–4
Montana	6–18	0–5, 19–21
Nebraska	0–21	—
Nevada	5–17	AI and VI at birth, MR at 3 Academically talented at 4
New Hampshire	3–21	—
New Jersey[c]	5–20	0–4, 21
New Mexico	5–21	—
New York	5–21	0–5
North Carolina	5–18	0–4, 18–21
North Dakota	6–21	3–5
Ohio	5–21	0–4
Oklahoma	0–21 Severely handicapped 4–21 Mildly handicapped	0–3 Mildly handicapped
Oregon	7–18	0–21
Pennsylvania	8–17	4.6–21
Rhode Island	3–21	—
South Carolina	6–21 (except HH 4–21)	5 (except HH)
South Dakota	In need of special assistance 3–21; prolonged assistance 0–21	—
Tennessee	4–21	0–21
Texas	3–21 (except 0–22 for HI, VI, DB)	3–22 (except HI, VI, DB)
Utah	5–21	0–4
Vermont	5–21	0–5
Virginia	2–21	0–2
Washington	6–21	0–5
West Virginia	5–23	3–4
Wisconsin	3–21	0–3
Wyoming	7–16	0–6

[c] As of 9/83, 3–21 mandated, 0–3 will be permissive.
This information was compiled and verified by the National Association of State Directors of Special Education.

state guidelines change from time to time. You may want to call the Director of Special Education from your local school system to find out if the guidelines in your state have changed since 1982, the time at which this chart was compiled.

If you want to know about your own state laws, you can get this information by requesting a copy of your state's regulations for educating handicapped children from the State Department of Education or by asking for it from the State Director of Special Education or a staffmember from the same office. The phone number of the State Director of Special Education can be obtained from the State Department of Education (referred to in some states as the Department of Public Instruction). If you find out that your state does not provide public education for 3–5-year-old handicapped children, then the following description of P.L. 94–142 and corresponding state law will not apply to your search for an appropriate preschool for your child. However, this information will be extremely useful when your child does reach public school age.

WHAT ARE THE MAJOR LEGAL REQUIREMENTS OF P.L. 94–142 AND OF CORRESPONDING STATE LAW?

The cornerstone of federal and state legislation is the provision of a *free appropriate public education* to handicapped children. There are numerous parts to this legislation that can be organized into six major principles. These principles include zero reject, nondiscriminatory evaluation, individualized education, least restrictive environment, due process, and parent participation. The legal requirement for a free appropriate public education is met when each of these principles is carried out with each handicapped child. It is very important for you to be aware of these principles and to understand your rights associated with each. The remaining portion of this chapter provides you with this information.

Zero Reject

Zero reject means that *all* handicapped children must be provided with educational services and that these services must be tailored to the individual needs of each student. If a child lives in a state with laws providing preschool services to handicapped children, then those preschool children must be provided with special education and related services.

The legal definitions for special education and related services are important for you to know. *Special education* is defined as:

Specially designed instruction, at no cost to the parent, to meet the unique needs of a handicapped child, including classroom instruction, instruction in physical education, home instruction, and instruction in hospitals and institutions.[19]

Two important parts of this definition are that the education must be free (e.g., at no cost to the parent) and that it may be provided in a variety of settings.

The zero reject principle also applies to *related services,* which are defined by P.L. 94–142 as follows:

Transportation and such developmental, corrective, and other supportive services as are required to assist a handicapped child to benefit from special education, and includes speech pathology and audiology, psychological services, physical and occupational therapy, recreation, early identification and assessment of disabilities in children, counseling services, and medical services for diagnostic or evaluation purposes. The term also includes school health services, social work services in schools, and parent counseling and training.[20]

The definitions of each of these services appear in Table 6.3. School systems are required by P.L. 94–142 to provide the full range of related services needed by handicapped children so that they can benefit from special education. If you are inter-

---

[19] *Federal Register.* 1977. August 23, 1977, p. 42480. U.S. Government Printing Office, Washington, DC.

[20] *Federal Register.* 1977. August 23, 1977, p. 42473. U.S. Government Printing Office, Washington, DC.

Table 6.3. Related services in special education

Program	Services
Audiology	a) Identification of children with hearing loss b) Determination of the range, nature, and degree of hearing loss, including referral for medical or other professional attention for the habilitation of hearing c) Provision of habilitative activities, such as language habilitation, auditory training, speech reading (lip reading), hearing evaluation, and speech conservation d) Creation and administration of programs for prevention of hearing loss e) Counseling and guidance of pupils, parents, and teachers regarding hearing loss f) Determination of the child's need for group and individual amplification, selecting and fitting an appropriate aid, and evaluating the effectiveness of amplification.
Counseling services	Services provided by qualified social workers, psychologists, guidance counselors, or other qualified personnel.
Early identification	Implementation of a formal plan for identifying a disability as early as possible in a child's life.
Medical services	Services provided by a licensed physician to determine a child's medically related handicapping condition, which results in the child's need for special education and related services.
Occupational therapy	a) Improving, developing, or restoring functions impaired or lost through illness, injury, or deprivation b) Improving ability to perform tasks for independent functioning when functions are impaired or lost c) Preventing through early intervention, initial or further impairment or loss of function.
Parent counseling and training	Assisting parents in understanding the special needs of their child and providing parents with information about child development.
Physical therapy	Services provided by a qualified physical therapist.

Continued

Table 6.3—*Continued*

Program	Services
Psychological services	a) Administering psychological and educational tests and other assessment procedures b) Interpreting assessment results c) Obtaining, integrating, and interpreting information about child behavior and conditions relating to learning. d) Consulting with other staff members in planning school programs to meet the special needs of children as indicated by psychological tests, interviews, and behavioral evaluations. e) Planning and managing a program of psychological services, including psychological counseling for children and parents.
Recreation	a) Assessment of leisure function b) Therapeutic recreation services c) Recreation programs in schools and community agencies d) Leisure education
School health services	Services provided by a qualified school nurse or other qualified person.
Social work services	a) Preparing a social or developmental history on a handicapped child b) Group and individual counseling with the child and family c) Working with those problems in a child's living situation (home, school, and community) that affect the child's adjustment in school d) Mobilizing school and community resources to enable the child to receive maximum benefit from his or her educational program.
Speech pathology	a) Identification of children with speech or language disorders b) Diagnosis and appraisal of specific speech or language disorders c) Referral for medical or other professional attention necessary for the habilitation of speech or language disorders

Table 6.3—*Continued*

Program	Services
	d) Provisions of speech and language services for the habilitation or prevention of communicative disorders
	e) Counseling and guidance of parents, children, and teachers regarding speech and language disorders.
Transportation	a) Travel to and from school and between schools
	b) Travel in and around school buildings
	c) Specialized equipment (such as special or adapted buses, lifts, and ramps) if required to provide special transportation for a handicapped child.

From: *Federal Register.* 1977, 42 (163).

ested in detailed information on the school system's responsibility for providing related services, you can find references in the resource section.

Some school systems may not be able to provide an appropriate special education or the full range of related services needed by a handicapped child. In these cases, the local school system must find an appropriate program and must pay for the full educational expenses and nonmedical care of the handicapped student. In cases in which a residential program (i.e., a school or institution where the child would live full-time) is necessary, the school system must pay for the room, board, and educational expenses for handicapped children within the age ranges of state guidelines (see Table 6.2). School systems that cannot provide the full range of services needed by the handicapped children in their districts may pay other agencies, such as the local mental health center, a neighboring school system, or a private clinic or agency, to provide the needed services to the handicapped children for whom they are responsible. This arrangement is frequently called *subcontracting*. The following situation illustrates the principle:

Rick was born with a severe hearing loss. When he reached age 4, his parents were very concerned that he receive a special education program emphasizing the development of language skills. In the small town in which he lives, Rick is the only preschool child with a hearing impairment. A neighboring school system has developed a comprehensive program for hearing impaired children with needs similar to Rick's. The Director of Special Education from Rick's community suggested to Rick's parents that the nearby program might be ideally suited for Rick. His parents visited the program and were quite impressed with the language and pre-academic skill training. Arrangements were worked out for the local school to pay the neighboring school system to provide services to Rick. This subcontract covered the financial costs of the program and daily transportation.

What is the role of the parent with regard to this principle of zero reject? A major responsibility of parents is to find out if their child can receive a free appropriate preschool education according to the laws of the state in which they reside. If the child can receive a free appropriate education, then the next step is for the parents and the public school officials to work together to decide what type of program would best meet the child's needs. A father of a preschool child offers this advice to other parents:

I made a big mistake in enrolling my child in a private preschool and then later learning that the state offers free services. I wrote the Director of Special Education and requested that the school pay the tuition at the private preschool. I was told that, because I placed my son in the private program, I was responsible for paying. I was told that I first must present my child to the school system for enrollment. If they could not adequately serve my child in a program, then a private placement would be made. They are responsible for paying only when they participate in the decision that placement in a private program is necessary.

To make the decision about the best type of program, the child's needs must be identified or assessed. This process is called *evaluation* and leads to the second principle of P.L. 94–142—

the needs of handicapped children must be identified in a non-discriminatory evaluation.

Nondiscriminatory Evaluation

Evaluation basically means that professionals make a judgment as to the child's educational needs. As part of this process, the child will be asked to perform certain tasks or will be given appropriate educational or developmental tests.

There are two purposes of evaluation, according to the legal definition: 1) to determine whether or not the child is handicapped, and 2) if so, to identify the nature and extent of the special education and related services needed by the child. Thus, evaluation procedures should identify the child's strengths and weaknesses as a beginning point for planning specially designed instruction. *Nondiscriminatory* means that this testing must be done in a way that is fair for the child.

There are many legal requirements as to how evaluations of handicapped children are to be conducted so that they are fair for the child. Some of these include giving the tests in the child's native language (i.e., if a child cannot speak English and is given an IQ test in English, the child is not fairly tested), giving at least two or more tests to determine an appropriate program, testing the child in *all* areas related to the suspected handicap, and involving a team of professionals rather than only one individual in giving tests and interpreting the results.

The law also states that parents have certain rights associated with their child's evaluation:

1. Before the child is evaluated for the first time by the public school system to determine whether or not a handicap exists, parents must be told about the evaluation in a written notice.

2. The parents must give their consent before the school can test a handicapped child for the first time. If the school wants to re-evaluate or retest the child at a later time, parent consent is not required. If changes are suggested as a result of the evaluation findings (i.e., the child is changed to another type of program), parents must be informed in a written notice. The notices to parents about such changes must include the following information: a list of the parents' legal rights, a description of the school's proposed plans to meet the needs of the child, a description of the evaluation results, and any other information considered by school officials in making their recommendations.

If parents are not satisfied with the evaluation conducted by the public schools, they can request that an independent evaluation (i.e., an evaluation given by a licensed examiner, such as a psychologist, outside of the school system) be completed on their child. The information from this independent evaluation must be considered by the school in making decisions about the child's classification as handicapped and about the nature and extent of special education and related services needed by the child. The schools must also pay for the independent evaluation unless they can prove in a due process hearing (discussed later in the chapter) that their evaluation is appropriate in identifying the child's educational needs. If parents do not feel that their child has received a fair evaluation, then it is their right to do something about this. Chapter 7 contains suggestions about how you can be involved in your child's evaluation. A mother describes how she obtained an independent evaluation:

Our daughter, Debbie, has always had significant language delays. At the age of 5 her distortions of sounds and vocabulary were similar to that of her younger brother who is 3. For several years, Debbie had almost constant ear infections that resulted in a temporary mild hearing loss. During those times, she could not adequately hear the sounds of words. She was evaluated by the public school and classified as learning disabled. My husband and I were shocked, to say the least. We had never considered the fact that her language problems would have this result. We believed that such a classification was totally ridiculous. After learning about our right to an independent evaluation, we wrote a letter to the Superintendent of schools and told him that we intended to pursue this evaluation and that we expected to send the bill to him. We told him that we were willing to request a due process hearing unless our request was honored. I don't think he particularly liked it, but he did agree to pay for the independent evaluation. As I look back, that was one of the best decisions we have ever made. Debbie was evaluated at a private clinic by a speech clinician, an audiologist, and a psychologist. Their results indicated that Debbie qualifies for special education because of her language delay; however, they were emphatic in stating that she does not have a learning disability. The school system accepted this independent report. Thank goodness we took the time to do this. Debbie has enough problems with language without having the further complication of another label.

Once parents are satisfied that their child's needs have been properly identified during the evaluation process, then the next step is for parents and school officials to sit down together and decide upon the best program to meet those needs. This leads to the third principle of P.L. 94–142—the development of the child's individualized education program.

Individualized Education Programs

In order to ensure that special education programs and related services provided by the public school system are responsive to the needs of handicapped children, federal and state legislation requires the development of an *individualized education program* or *IEP*. There are two major parts to the IEP requirements: the IEP document and IEP meeting.

IEP Document

The *IEP document* outlines each handicapped child's educational program. Each IEP must include the following information:

1. The student's current level of educational performance
2. Annual goals or the progress expected within one calendar year
3. Short-term objectives, which are the small steps leading to the mastery of annual goals
4. The particular special education and related services that will be provided to the child

5. A description of the amount of time a child will be in the regular education program with nonhandicapped children
6. The dates when special education services will begin and will be terminated
7. How, when, and in what way the staff will use evaluation procedures to determine mastery of short-term objectives. Evaluation of the child's progress must be done at least on an annual basis.

An IEP must be developed for every child classified as handicapped and in need of special education and related services. Special education is defined as "specially designed instruction," regardless of whether the instruction is delivered in a regular classroom attended mostly by nonhandicapped children or in a special education class attended only by handicapped children. The decision as to whether instruction for the child needs to be specially designed should be made by comparing the handicapped child's instructional needs to typical instructional practices for nonhandicapped children at the same age and grade level. Careful thought should be given to a broad range of each child's needs, as discussed in Chapter 2. These needs include language development, motor development, self-help skills, socialization skills, adaptive behavior, self-concept, and pre-academic skills. (A sample IEP is included in Chapter 7.) The IEP must be completed by the beginning of the school year. Although "beginning of the school year" is not defined by law, local policy frequently requires IEP completion by October 1. Another legal requirement is that IEPs must be reviewed at least once on a yearly basis. As reported by a parent, the IEP can have many benefits:

My son, who is mentally retarded, is now in the second grade. He had his first IEP when he was 4 years old, so my husband and I have been attending conferences for 4 years. Working with the teachers to develop the IEP and then having our own copy has helped us to keep up with Vic's progress. Most parents tape their children's artwork to the refrigerator, but would you believe that that's where we put Vic's IEP? Every time he brings home papers we look to see which objectives he's working on. Another real plus is that we have a much clearer idea of how we can help him at home. My daughter started kindergarten this year. She's a normal child so she doesn't get an IEP. In many ways, I feel locked out of knowing about her program. I wish all kids would have IEPs.

Both the initial development of the IEP and the yearly review of it are completed within the context of an IEP meeting, which is discussed in the next section.

IEP Meeting

The purpose of the *IEP meeting* is to provide an opportunity for school staff and parents (and in many cases for older handicapped students) to decide together about the nature of the child's educational program. The school system is required to take steps to ensure that the following persons are present at the IEP meeting:

1. A representative of the school system (other than the student's teacher) who has qualifications to provide or to supervise special education
2. The child's teacher
3. One or both of the child's parents
4. Other persons, at the request of the parents or school personnel
5. For handicapped children who have been evaluated for the first time, either a person who evaluated the child must be present at the meeting or another person must be present (i.e., a representative of the school system or the child's teacher) who knows about the evaluation procedures used with the child and is familiar with the results.

Sample topics of discussion at the IEP meeting include annual goals, short-term objectives, and the type of special education and related service that are tailored to the child's individual needs.

The presence of parents is an important part of the IEP meeting. The school staff working with the handicapped child are required to tell parents of the purpose, time, location, and participants at the IEP meeting early enough so that parents will have an opportunity to come to this meeting. The school staff must also schedule the meeting at a mutually agreed upon time and place and give a copy of the child's IEP to the parents if they request one.

In some cases, as previously described, school systems sub-contract with private agencies (such as mental health centers) to provide special education programs to handicapped children. However, it should be pointed out that if the school system is legally responsible for serving handicapped children in the age range of 3–5, then they must assume responsibility for the development of the child's IEP and for carrying out the IEP. The following example illustrates this relation:

Karen is a four-year-old child who is multiply handicapped. Her local school system is required to serve handicapped children beginning at the age of four. The mental health center in Karen's community had been providing an excellent preschool program to multiply handicapped children for several years prior to the implementation of state law requiring the public school systems to serve young handicapped children. The school system therefore made the decision to subcontract with the local mental health center for services rather than to start another class for multiply handicapped children. The Director of Special Education from the local school worked with the staff from the mental health center in planning and conducting a comprehensive evaluation to identify Karen's educational needs.

Least Restrictive Environment

Federal and state laws require that handicapped children be educated in the *least restrictive environment.* This means that, to the maximum extent appropriate, handicapped children should be educated with children who are not handicapped. The placement of handicapped children in special classes or special schools should occur only when the nature or severity of the handicap prevents them from successfully being educated in regular classes with the use of supplementary aids and services. Supplementary aids and services include things like special materials as well as consultations between the preschool teacher and a specialist in the area of the child's disability.

The legal regulations state that school systems must provide a full range of educational placements from most restrictive, such as institutions, to least restrictive, such as regular classrooms. The members of the IEP committee should be able to decide which type of placement (i.e., which classroom or school) is best suited for each handicapped child.

Another requirement more applicable to school-age handicapped children associated with the least restrictive principle is that handicapped children should be educated in the same school they would attend if they were not handicapped (unless the IEP requires a different arrangement). They also have the right to participate in nonacademic (e.g., physical education) and extracurricular services (e.g., the school chorus and clubs) to the extent that is appropriate for each handicapped student.

Due Process

Due process is a way of making sure that parents and educators make fair decisions about the identification, evaluation, and placement of handicapped children. The phrase "due process" comes from the Fifth and Fourteenth Amendments of the Constitution, in which all citizens of this country are ensured due process of law before they are deprived of life, liberty, or property. In the context of educating handicapped children, due process requirements of federal and state law provide a system of checks and balances for the decisions of both parents and educators.

Several of the due process rights are associated with the nondiscriminatory evaluation procedures that are discussed earlier in this chapter in the section on evaluation. These rights include getting consent from parents before the initial evaluation is given for the purpose of classifying a child as handicapped, giving a written notice to parents any time the child is subsequently evaluated, and allowing parents to have an independent evaluation (administered by someone outside of the school system) of their handicapped child. The purpose of these due process safeguards is to make sure that children are fairly evaluated by the schools.

Another feature of the due process requirements is the right of parents and educators to challenge the decisions made by each other. Decisions can be formally challenged through the means of a *due process hearing.* Any denial of federal or state legal rights to a handicapped child or to parents can be addressed through such a hearing. An issue that could lead to a due process hearing brought by parents is leaving the handicapped child out of a preschool program run by the public school system when the state in which the child resides requires that such services be offered. Another such issue for a due process hearing could be the unwillingness on the part of the school to provide the number and type of related services needed by a given handicapped child.

A due process hearing is carried out by an impartial hearing officer. Impartial means that this person is fair and not biased toward either the parent or the school system. This officer may not be an employee of the school system. The hearing basically involves allowing both the parents and the educators to state issues of concern about the appropriateness of the child's education and to give evidence to support their concerns. After considering the evidence, the hearing officer makes a decision about the best way to make sure that the child is provided with an appropriate education.

Many regulations determine how due process hearings are conducted. These include the following rights of parents: they may be advised by a lawyer, they may present evidence, they may cross-examine witnesses, they may obtain a verbatim record of the hearing, they may obtain a written decision, and they may appeal the final decision of the hearing officer if they are dissatisfied with it. A due process hearing is only necessary when parents and educators have not been able to reach agreement in the IEP conference. Most parents of handicapped children will never be involved in a due process hearing; however, it is still important for parents to know that they have the right to make formal complaints against the school system. Chapter 12 contains more information on the role of parents in due process hearings. Names and descriptions of additional resource materials for parents on the topic of due process are included in the resource section.

Parent Participation

The last principle of federal and state legislation is *parent participation* in decision making. Each of the principles already described extends rights and responsibilities to parents, such as giving consent for evaluation, taking part in the IEP conference, and calling for a due process hearing. Parent participation is included as a separate principle to highlight it as a major theme of legislative requirements. It is also separate because some of the requirements to involve parents cannot be classified under any of the other five principles.

Parents have the right to look over all education records that the school has in their child's file. The right to review the records includes the following: parents have the right to read the records, to request that someone explain the contents of the records, and to request that the information in the records be changed because of inaccuracies or violations of privacy. The only exception to these rights is in situations in which parental rights are lost under state law concerning matters like guardianship, separation, and divorce.

Aside from parents, no one else legally may look at these records except for school staff responsible for educating the child. If someone else does want to have access to records (i.e., someone conducting research on preschool education), parents must receive a letter explaining the purpose for such release and they must give their written consent. As stated by a mother of a handicapped child: "I expect Stephen's teachers to be very careful about educational records. Let's face it, it's no one's business but the family's and the teacher's that Stephen is handicapped."

Thus, parents have the right of confidentiality of information pertaining to their handicapped child. They can control to whom and at what time information may be released.

PARENT AND CHILD RIGHTS IN P.L. 94–142

For the parent of a child who has been identified as having a handicap, the following rights are provided through federal legislation (P.L. 94–142):

1. A free appropriate public education with necessary related services to meet your child's needs (e.g., speech therapy, physical therapy, counseling, and transportation) must be provided by your school system.

2. Your child must be given a comprehensive evaluation for the purpose of identifying whether a handicap exists and for pinpointing strengths and weaknesses as the basis for planning an individualized education program.

3. Your child may not receive an initial evaluation in order to be placed in a special education program unless you are previously informed and you voluntarily give your consent. You may withdraw your decision to give consent at any time.

4. You are entitled to receive an explanation of all evaluation results and an explanation of any action proposed or rejected in regard to evaluation results.

5. You have the right to request an independent evaluation conducted by someone outside of the school and to have the results considered in discussions regarding the placement of your child.

6. An individualized education program (IEP) must be developed that identifies the nature of the specially designed instruction that is needed by your child.

7. You have the right to participate actively in the development of your child's individualized education program (IEP).

8. Your child should be educated in classes with children who do not have handicaps if such classes are appropriate to the needs of your child. This means, for example, that your child may not be removed from regular class placement to be put in a special class attended only by handicapped children unless you and the school personnel believe that the special class would be the best placement.

9. You have the right to request an objective hearing (due process hearing) at any time when you disagree with the proposed procedures for evaluation and/or placement of your child. At the hearing you may have legal counsel, may present evidence, may cross-examine witnesses, and may obtain written findings of the proceedings.

10. The privacy of all school records must be maintained. You may request copies of your child's school records. Furthermore, you may obtain information from the chairperson of the special services committee concerning the particular individuals who are allowed to see your child's records.
11. You may look at all educational records and request explanations of information contained in the records. You may also request the information to be changed if you do not agree with it.

SUMMARY

The major principles and regulations of federal and state legislation are the foundation upon which special education practices are based. It is important for you to know your rights and those of your child. These rights are summarized above. Another important consideration to keep in mind is that, when this book went to press, attempts were being made by the Reagan administration to reduce the P.L. 94–142 regulations. At the time of this writing, no changes have been made. It is impossible to predict the future course of events. We wholeheartedly believe that the principles and regulations represent good professional standards in the field of special education. We urge you to consider the meaning of these legal rights for you and for your child and to express your viewpoints to your senators and representatives at both the federal and state levels.

Chapter 7

WHAT IS YOUR ROLE IN YOUR CHILD'S EVALUATION AND IEP MEETING?

No law works unless people like you make sure that it does what it is supposed to do. The purpose of this chapter is to look at two areas in which you have the right to be involved: in the evaluation of your child and in the development of the individualized education program. Your participation can make a crucial difference in ensuring that your child receives an appropriate education.

The individualized education program, which is often called the IEP, is the backbone of your child's education. It specifies in writing what is appropriate for your child in terms of the classroom placement, the goals and objectives to be taught, the related services to be provided, and other things that you and the school representatives believe are important to ensure an appropriate education for your child. The IEP is reviewed and rewritten each year to keep up with your child's changing needs. Working with professionals, parents play a major role in developing the child's IEP. The mother of a kindergartener who is mentally retarded shares this perspective on IEPs:

I was really unsure of myself when I went to my first IEP conference two years ago. The teachers and psychologist discussed Michael's goals and objectives with me, and it seemed like I was hit with an awful lot of information at once. After participating in several IEP conferences, I can honestly say I have learned a lot. I write out notes ahead of time to make sure I remember to say everything on my mind. I believe the IEP meeting is one of the most important ways parents can be involved. It is the opportunity for me to make sure that Michael is getting what he needs.

STEPS TOWARD GETTING AN IEP FOR YOUR CHILD

Step 1: Referral

The first step is to make sure that your child is identified to the school system as having a special need. This is a rather straightforward step. You, your pediatrician, or anyone who knows your child should call your local school system, report that you think your child has a special need, and request that your child be evaluated. At this point you may want to set up an appointment with the director of special education, with early childhood specialists, or with a school psychologist to discuss your child's needs. You may be familiar with Child Find, which is a project in every state set up to identify children under six years of age with special needs. Projects like Child Find reflect the importance placed upon making sure that families of children with special needs receive support as soon as possible. The way to get this support is to let the school officials know about your child.

Step 2: Evaluation

During the evaluation, school representatives will meet with you and your child as a way of understanding your child's special needs. One of the major purposes of the evaluation will be to identify your child's strengths and weaknesses, as a basis for planning the IEP. Here are some areas of your child's development that might be examined by professionals through tests, by

talking with you, and by spending time with your child:
1. Motor development (walking, running, and balancing)
2. Language development (talking, communicating, and vocalization)
3. Socialization (getting along with others and separating from parents)
4. Hearing and vision.

Initially, all areas should be examined to provide a comprehensive understanding of your child's strengths and weaknesses. In the next section of this chapter, outlines are provided to show how you and the professionals evaluating your child can work together to ensure that this evaluation process goes well.

Step 3: The IEP Conference

After the evaluation it is time for you and the school representatives to get together and plan your child's IEP. The intent of the legal requirements for parent involvement is that you and school representatives should be equal participants in deciding upon the best educational plan for your child. Remember, your knowledge and observations of your child are as important if not *more* important than are test scores. Your observations and assessment of preschool options in your community are based on that knowledge; therefore, you are probably in the best situation to know what the best plan is for your child and for your family. This conference is described more completely in the last section of this chapter, and ways in which your participation can be enhanced are also suggested.

YOUR INVOLVEMENT IN YOUR CHILD'S EVALUATION

Why Your Involvement Is Important

Playing an active part in your child's evaluation is important for two reasons. First, professionals can learn much about your child from you. You know more about what your child can and cannot do on a daily basis than does anyone else. You can provide information on your child's developmental history (i.e., at what age did he or she begin to talk) and information from previous reports of other professionals who might have evaluated or worked with your child. You also have some idea about how your child can best respond to the evaluator. All of this information can be extremely helpful and can contribute to a more accurate understanding of your child's needs.

Second, you can learn from the person doing the evaluation. This is an opportunity to receive detailed information about your child's strengths and weaknesses. You might learn more about the educational terms used to describe certain skills (Table 2.1 in Chapter 2 contains an outline of some of these terms). You can also learn about the tests that are used and the way in which professionals gather information in order to make specific recommendations. To do this, you need to ask questions before, during, and after the evaluation to clarify the meaning of certain findings. The major reason why this evaluation process is important is that the results will be used as the basis for developing the IEP. Thus, it is important for you to make sure that the evaluation is as accurate as possible and that you have an understanding of the results. Being part of your child's evaluation is considered to be so important that federal and state law spell out certain rights that you have in this respect. These specific rights are enumerated in Chapter 6.

It is important to remember that if your do not agree with the evaluation results, do not go ahead with the IEP conference. Because the evaluation will play an important part in IEP development, you have a right to delay this meeting until you believe your child has received a fair evaluation. As discussed in Chapter 6, you may request an independent evaluation to be conducted by someone not employed by the school system if you are not satisfied with the comprehensiveness or the accuracy of the school's evaluation. This independent evaluation must be paid for by the school system, unless they can document the appropriateness of their own evaluation through a due process hearing.

Suggestions for Your Involvement in the Evaluation Process

Research has suggested that going through the evaluation process with a young child can be a stressful event for parents. One

father describes the experience of observing his mentally retarded son's evaluation: "It was a terribly stressful day. Observing
Jim's failure on test after test was like being beat over the head
with the severity and sadness of the whole situation."

Numerous articles have been written for professionals with
suggestions for ways they can effectively carry out an evaluation. The primary focus for many of these articles is the importance of making sure that a two-way communication system is
set up between parents and professionals during the evaluation
process. This means that there must be a free flow of information, whereby parents and professionals can share ideas and can
learn from each other. When this takes place effectively, then
the evaluation can benefit everyone involved.

There are certain steps that you can take before, during,
and after the evaluation that may help ensure that the evaluation
process goes as smoothly as possible.[21]

I. Before the Evaluation

A. Identify both the difficult and the manageable aspects of
   previous evaluations and talk to other parents about their
   experiences.
B. Talk with your spouse, with your child's therapist or teacher,
   or with an earlier evaluator about how your child handles
   evaluations in various areas, such as:
   1. reactions to strangers
   2. tolerance for testing demands
   3. ability to sit still for long periods
   4. fatigue threshold (how long until the child gets too tired
      to work at his or her best)
   5. need for an interpreter if non-English-speaking child or a
      user of sign language
   6. ability to separate from you, and to leave and stay with a
      stranger
   7. high and low points in the day.
C. Talk with your child about prior evaluation experiences and

---

[21] Anderson, W., Chitwood, S., and Hayden, D. 1981. *Negotiating the Special
Education Maze.* Spectrum Books, Englewood Cliffs, NJ. Many of the suggestions for
involvement in the evaluation process are adapted from this book.

about what to expect from this one. Provide an opportunity for your child to ask questions and to express feelings.

D. Find out about the evaluation facility's expectations for your participation and consider various roles you might choose or need to assume, such as:
1. observer of your child
2. active participant in testing
3. supporter and comforter to your child
4. information source about your child.

E. Make a list of your questions and prioritize your concerns about the evaluation. Set up a meeting with the evaluators to discuss your questions and concerns. Seek the clarification you need in order to feel comfortable with the evaluation process.

F. Take your child on a pre-evaluation visit to explore the evaluation facility and to meet the persons who will be giving the tests. This step is particularly important if your child is severely handicapped in some way and cannot benefit from verbal explanations or conversations about what to expect.

G. Give your child the chance to make some choices on the day of the evaluation, such as: what to wear, what to take for a snack, and what toy or book to take.

II. During the Evaluation

A. When you arrive for the evaluation:
1. Familiarize your child with the areas he or she will be in (e.g., waiting room, playroom, testing room, and restroom).
2. Introduce your child to one or two of the adults with whom the child will be working.
3. Review the day's plan with your child.
4. Encourage your child to ask questions and share concerns.

B. If you are interested in observing the testing, request that you be permitted to do so. While observing, record your impressions of your child's performances and your impressions of the way in which the evaluator is relating to your child.

C. Watch for fatigue and stress signals from your child.

D. Ask for explanations of any procedures that are unclear to you.

E. Ensure that your child has an opportunity to take breaks for rest, refreshment, and toileting.

III. After the Evaluation

A. Ask the evaluators when you can expect to be informed of the results and the way in which they will inform you (e.g., written report or conference). Also let them know your preferences and make a decision on a schedule and strategy that is agreeable to all parties.

B. Encourage your child to review the experience through storytelling, pictures, or dramatic play.

C. Review your notes on the evaluation and anticipate your child's strengths and weaknesses as evidenced in this evaluation.

D. Set up a meeting to review the results with the evaluator. This meeting may be held strictly to discuss evaluation findings, or a report of evaluation results may be incorporated into the IEP meeting.

E. Note your concerns in the form of questions to be asked at the evaluation or IEP conference.

F. Obtain written reports of this evaluation and review them to see that they are:

1. accurate

2. complete

3. bias free

4. jargon free

5. current

6. consistent

7. understandable.

G. Inform your child of the evaluation results—what was learned about strengths and needs—with consideration for the child's ability to comprehend the findings.

H. Check the actual experience against what you had anticipated. If you are so inclined, write a letter to the person in charge of the evaluation facility describing your sense of the positive and, perhaps, negative aspects of the process.

YOUR INVOLVEMENT IN THE DEVELOPMENT OF YOUR CHILD'S IEP

Why Your Involvement Is Important

Research on parent participation in IEP meetings has indicated that being prepared for this meeting can make a difference in how actively parents participate in decision making. As one mother explains:

I'm not a very assertive person. The first time I went to an IEP conference I don't think I said a thing. When I was driving home from the meeting, I was angry at myself for not speaking up. Before the next meeting, I asked my neighbor to go with me. We made a list of the questions that were on our minds. We even sat at the kitchen table and practiced asking each other questions to help us build up our confidence. The conference went very smoothly. Also, I felt better about myself.

One way to be prepared is to have a clear understanding of the legal requirements associated with the IEP. These laws are outlined in Chapter 6. Another way to prepare yourself is to be familiar with the placement options that might be considered in the IEP meeting. One mother recounts:

We knew we had to get ready for next fall when Annie was going to move from her early intervention program to public school kindergarten. This spring I started my own private investigation. I visited the regular kindergarten classrooms in our neighborhood school and ruled out those placements immediately. The regular teachers and the one resource teacher for the school were overwhelmed by children with behavior problems. I knew they wouldn't have the time to deal with a visually impaired child. Then I looked at the EMR (educable mentally retarded) classroom in a nearby school. In the one hour and ten minutes during which I observed the class, the teacher did not make one positively reinforcing statement. There were no materials suitable for a child like Annie, and what was worse was that in talking with the teacher I did not feel she was capable of making the kinds of adaptations that I felt were crucial for Annie's success in a classroom. I was terrified! The one hope I could cling to was the IEP. I started making notes then on what I felt Annie needed in a learning environment in order to succeed. What shocked me the most in looking at classrooms and talking to teachers was how little they know about working with blind or with partially sighted children. I realized that what was desperately needed was a visual consultant to work with the teachers and to work with Annie. I spelled out all of this in the IEP conference a few weeks ago. Now if things don't get done in the fall, I can go back and say, "It's laid out for you in the IEP, and the bargain is not being met on your side." I'm waiting to see if they come up with the visual consultant—they've said they're working on it. [Through the efforts of this mother and of other parents of visually impaired students, the school system now has a visual consultant.]

A sample IEP is included in Figure 7.1. This IEP was developed in an infant treatment program for a one-year-old child with cerebral palsy. It covers cognitive and gross motor skill areas. You may want to look this over before reading about the IEP conference.

Suggestions for Your Involvement in the IEP Conference

Exactly how IEP conferences are carried out varies from school system to school system. It is important to find out the procedure used by your school system so that you can avoid the kind of stressful meeting described by Ken Yockey:[22]

Barb [wife] was told that before Debbie actually could be enrolled in a specific program, the school

---

[22] Yockey, K., 1983. Facing the inquisition. In: T. Dougan, L. Isbell, and P. Vyas (eds.), *We Have Been There: A Guidebook for Parents of People with Mental Retardation.* Abingdon Press, Nashville, TN.

Figure 7.1.   Individualized education program. (Reprinted with permission from Turnbull, A.P., Strickland, B., and Brantley, J.C. 1982. *Developing and Implementing Individualized Education Programs.* 2nd Ed., pp. 121–125. Charles E. Merrill Publishing Co., Columbus, OH.)

Identification Information

Student's Name: Shane W.   Birthdate: 1–19–79
School: Rosewood   Parents' Name: Stephen and Valerie W.
Grade/Placement: Infant Treatment Program   Address: 320 W. 19th St.
                                                               Phone: (Home) 621–0662   (Business) 621–9792

Medical Information

Vision: Within normal limits   Hearing: Within normal limits (December 13, 1979)

Medication: None

Physical Condition: Extremely hypotonic, quadriplegic cerebral palsied. Frequent problems with upper respira-
                    tory infections and ear infections.

Schedule of Services

Monday	Tuesday	Wednesday	Thursday	Friday
		9:30–10:00 Group Time (Art or Music)		9:30–10:00 Group Time (Art or Music)
		10–11:30 Individual lessons in cognitive, gross motor areas		10–11:30 Individual lessons in cognitive, gross motor areas
		11:30–12:00 Snack (self-help) with mother		11:30–12:00 Snack (self-help) with mother

Comments

Infant Treatment Group meets only on Wednesday and Friday morning. The group helps show the parents effective ways to work with their children and helps the parent devise objectives to work on at home.

Committee Members

Teacher:

LEA Representative

Parents:

Other:

Date of Beginning Service: 3–19–1980
Projected Ending Date: 3–1981
Date IEP Initially Approved: 3–14–1980
Review Date: 6–1–1980; 9–1–1980; 1–8–1981

TESTING INFORMATION

Student's Name: Shane

Test Name	Name of Tester	Date Admin./ General Results
Carolina Curriculum for Handicapped Infants (a curriculum-referenced checklist, which accompanies the curriculum used at the Infant Treatment Group)	January 25, 1980	* Fine motor—Shane is developing at an almost age-appropriate rate in this area. He has a nice superior pincer grasp. He responds positively to most tactile stimulation activities. His reaction and grasp are well directed, although it takes him a long time to reach objects placed at arm's length sometimes (12 month level). * Gross motor— a) prone—Shane is just developing the ability to lift his head in this position. He works best over a wedge (2–3 month level).
Adaptive Performance Instrument	January 30, 1980	* Fine motor—well-directed reach, good pincer grasp. * Gross motor—beginning to be able to hold up head in prone; ability to hold head steady when upright is also emerging. * Social skills—not very "people oriented"—developing a stronger attachment to his mother. * Language skills—ability to produce a variety of vowel-consonant sounds. Has differential cries his mother can understand. * Cognitive—object permanence is not well established.

b) supine—Shane's preferred position. He is developing the ability to roll from this position (3 month level).

c) upright—Shane is developing the ability to lift his head upright for longer periods of time in this position. He does not have much trunk awareness in this position (2–3 month level).

* Language skills—

a) receptive—Shane does not consistently respond to his own name yet. He is beginning to understand "up" and "bye." He is not particularly attentive to the human voice (6–7 month level).

b) expressive—Shane vocalizes a variety of vowel and consonant sounds, but he vocalizes very frequently. He occasionally repeats sounds made by his caregiver that are already in his repertoire (5–6 month level).

* Cognitive—Shane has an inconsistent understanding of object permanence. Shane likes games and is beginning to anticipate frequently occurring events in a game he plays with his mother.

Name of Student: Shane

Subject Area: Gross Motor

Present Level of Educational Functioning	Annual Goals/Criteria	Instructional Objectives/Criteria	Date Achieved
I. Shane is beginning to consistently lift his head or turn his head to the side when he is placed in prone. When over a wedge or a person's knee while in the prone position, Shane is inconsistently able to lift his head and chest up far enough to look around. He still tires quickly in this position, however.	I. In a prone position, Shane will be able to support himself on his hands with his arms extended and his head upright for $\geq$ 30 seconds, 4/5 times on 5 consecutive days.	1. Shane, when placed in a prone position, will consistently lift his head and free his nose, 5/5 times on 3 consecutive days.	[05/80]
		2. With a wedge, or prone over a person's knee, Shane will lift himself on his elbows, $\geq$ 30 seconds, 5/5 times on 3 consecutive days.	[08/80]
		3. Shane will lift his head to a 45° angle; supporting himself on his elbows for $\geq$ 30 seconds, 5/5 times on 3 consecutive days.	[11/80]

II. Shane's ability to roll from his back to his stomach is improving rapidly. He is able to perform this roll fairly consistently, although it often takes him a long time. Shane is not able to roll over completely when placed upon his stomach.

II. Shane will be able to roll smoothly from his back to his back, 5/5 times on 3 consecutive days.

[05/80]

1. Shane will roll from his stomach to his back or vice-versa by arching his back, 5/5 times on 3 consecutive days.

[08/80]

2. Shane will roll from his back to his stomach and return to his back again when placed on a moderate incline, 5/5 times on 3 consecutive days.

[11/80]

3. Shane will roll from his stomach to his back quickly and readily; leading with an arm or leg and showing trunk rotation, 5/5 times on 3 consecutive days.

Name of Student: Shane

Subject Area: Gross Motor

Present Level of Educational Functioning	Annual Goals/Criteria	Instructional Objectives/Criteria	Date Achieved
III. Shane is able to hold his head erect when he is held upright. After several minutes of being upright, Shane's head tends to wobble a bit. Shane is able to hold his head steady inconsistently when the person holding him sways about. Shane can hold his trunk steady for very brief periods of time when in an upright position. (* Note—Shane should not work in the sitting position until he has mastered Gross Motor goals I.3 and III.3.)	III. Shane, when placed in a sitting position will be able to sit unsupported for 1 minute, 4/5 times on 5 consecutive days.	1. Shane will be able to maintain his head erect and steady for 1 minute as adult holding him sways back and forth, 5/5 times on 3 consecutive days.	[06/80]
		2. Shane will hold his trunk steady without support while being held for ≥ 30 seconds, 5/5 times on 3 consecutive days.	[09/80]
		3. Shane will maintain trunk steadiness and balance while adult holding him sways back and forth for 60 seconds, 5/5 times on 3 consecutive days.	[12/80]

Name of Student: <u>Shane</u>

Subject Area: Cognitive

Present Level of Educational Functioning	Annual Goals/Criteria	Instructional Objectives/Criteria	Date Achieved
I. Shane inconsistently watches people talking and/or gesturing. Shane inconsistently imitates gestures he is already known to perform if they are imitated by the caregiver. (Example: will shake a bell following the caregiver shaking the bell.)	I. Shane will imitate new activities that are modeled for him by an adult, 5/5 times for the same activity on 3 consecutive days.	1. Shane will look at person talking and/or gesturing, 5/5 times on 3 consecutive days.	[06/80]
		2. Shane will continue an activity he is performing if it is imitated by the caregiver 3/4 times on 3 consecutive days.	[07/80]
		3. Shane will begin an activity already in his repertoire if the same activity is begun by his caregiver, 3/4 times on 2 consecutive days.	[09/80]
		4. Shane will approximately imitate an activity when his action is visible to himself, 3/4 times on 2 consecutive days.	[11/80]

Name of Student: Shane

Subject Area: Cognitive

Present Level of Educational Functioning	Annual Goals/Criteria	Instructional Objectives/Criteria	Date Achieved
		5. Shane will imitate unfamiliar activities that are out of sight of his body, 3/4 times on 2 consecutive days.	[01/81]
II. Shane likes to play games like patty-cake. He sometimes smiles, vocalizes, or moves about when playing games with an adult. He anticipates when his mother will tickle him in their "I'm gonna get-cha" game, but he has not generalized this skill to other people or other games yet.	II. Shane will initiate activities with adults by starting movements at least 1 time per day on 5 different days.	1. Shane will anticipate (demonstrated through vocalization or movement) frequently occurring events in games or nursery rhymes, 3/5 times on 2 consecutive days.	[05/80]
		2. Shane will repeat activities that get interesting results/reactions from others, repeats for 3 different behaviors, for at least 2 different days.	[08/80]
		3. Shane will get an adult to continue an activity by starting body movements at least 2 times per day for 5 consecutive days.	[11/80]

Name of Student: Shane

Subject Area: Cognitive

Present Level of Educational Functioning	Annual Goals/Criteria	Instructional Objectives/Criteria	Date Achieved
III. Shane usually shakes most of the toys placed in his hands. He is currently learning to squeeze a squeaker toy.	III. Shane will demonstrate different activities with toys having obviously different properties; 5 appropriate activities with 5 different toys on 3 separate days.	1. Shane commonly performs 2 or more activities with objects, 2 or more activities on 3 separate days.	[05/80]
		2. Shane commonly performs 3 or more activities with objects, 3 or more activities on 3 separate days.	[07/80]
		3. Shane commonly performs 4 or more activities with objects, 4 or more activities on 3 separate days.	[09/80]
		4. Shane explores toys and responds to their differences, 5 successful trials on 3 separate days.	[11/80]

district conducted something called a "placement interview," the purpose being to explain the programs to the parents, to get some personal background information on the child, and, as a result, to ensure the most appropriate placement for that child. Both Barb and I were quite impressed.

Our appointment was set for mid-afternoon, not a particularly convenient time for most fathers. It has occurred to me since that these interviews might just be set at such inconvenient hours specifically to discourage participation by both parents, but then, maybe I've gotten a little paranoid. By pure coincidence my job situation at the time was such that I could take an afternoon off without any problem. I am certainly glad now that I didn't use the inconvenience of the hour as an excuse for not going (I had used that excuse frequently in the past). It turned out to be an interesting experience, one I am unlikely to forget.

Quite frankly, Barb and I had been expecting a rather informal meeting with a placement specialist, the teacher, and perhaps a psychologist to talk a little bit about Debbie and the programs available at the school. What we encountered was something quite different. When we arrived, the principal ushered us into a small, narrow room with a single, long table about which were seated no less than seven people. The principal proceeded to introduce the placement officer, the teacher, a doctor, a nurse, a social worker, a speech therapist, and a consultant psychologist (apparently the janitor had a previous engagement). I wondered, briefly, whether these people suspected Barb and me of being emotionally unstable, or that we might exhibit violent, antisocial behavioral tendencies, or both, because they outnumbered us four-to-one (we were, after all, parents of a mentally retarded child). It was with no small relief that I noted that the women were all somewhat frail, and the men were all nearly twice my age.

It is clear that the potential positive aspects of having a

large number of professionals involved in an IEP conference may be negated if parents are not prepared for their presence.

Generally, conferences can be described as consisting of six components:

1. preconference preparation
2. initial conference proceedings
3. interpretation of evaluation results
4. development of goals, objectives, and related services
5. decision about preschool placement and related services
6. conclusion of the meeting.

Ways for enhancing your involvement in each of these parts of the conference are provided below:[23]

I. Preconference Preparation

A. Ensure that the time of meeting is convenient. Reschedule the meeting if the time suggested by the school personnel is inconvenient.
B. Obtain any information that you believe will be helpful at the meeting, including your child's records from previous evaluations.
C. If possible, plan for both parents to attend the meeting.
D. Ask an advocate or friend to attend the meeting with you if their presence would make you more comfortable.
E. Make a list of any questions that you would like answered at the meeting.
F. Inform the school of your intent to attend the meeting and the persons whom you will bring with you. State your eagerness to be involved in the decisions pertaining to your child's program.

II. Initial Conference Proceedings

A. If you are not introduced at the meeting to any persons you do not know, introduce yourself to all committee members.

---

[23] Turnbull, A.P., and Strickland, B. 1981. Parents and the educational system. In: J.L. Paul (ed.), *Understanding and Working with Parents of Children with Special Needs*. Holt, Rinehart & Winston, Inc., New York. The outline for enhancing your involvement in the IEP conference is adapted from this book.

B. Ask questions to clarify the particular role of other committee members if this is not explained initially.

C. If you bring a friend or advocate, introduce them and explain their role.

D. If you have a time limit for the meeting, let other committee members know.

E. Ask the chairperson to state the purpose of the meeting and to review the agenda, if this is not done.

F. If you have any questions about your legal rights, ask for a clarification.

III. Interpretation of Evaluation Results

A. Ensure that the psychologist or the other evaluators state all tests that were administered and the specific results of each.

B. You may make a record for yourself or ask for a written copy of the test results and of the evaluation of your child. This may become an important part of your records on your child.

C. Ensure that the education implications of the evaluation results are identified.

D. Ensure that your child's needs, as you have identified them, have been assessed during the evaluation. If some of your child's needs have not been addressed, you should ask that further evaluation be done.

E. If any professional jargon is used that you do not understand, ask for a clarification.

F. Ask how your child was classified in regard to a particular handicapping condition (e.g., mental retardation or learning disability).

G. If you disagree with evaluation findings or with a classification, state your disagreement.

H. If your disagreement cannot be resolved within the meeting, ask for an independent evaluation to be administered by a psychologist or by an appropriate professional outside the school.

I. Do not proceed with the development of the IEP until you and the school personnel agree on your child's evaluation results.

IV. Development of Goals, Objectives, and Evaluation Procedures

A. If the evaluator's description of your child's performance is not as you perceive it, do give your description of his or her performance level.

B. State the skills and content areas that you believe are most important for your child's program.

C. If you question the goals and objectives suggested by the school, ask for justification.

D. Ensure that *all* skill areas requiring specially designed instruction are included in the IEP.

E. Clarify the manner in which the responsibility for teaching the objectives will be shared among the teachers and related service providers.

F. If you are willing to assume responsibility for teaching or for reviewing some of the objectives with the child, make this known to the committee.

G. Ensure that the types of evaluation to be used to assess mastery of your child's objectives are specified.

V. Placement Decision and Related Services

A. State the placement (regular preschool or specialized preschool) that you believe is most appropriate for your child.

B. Be sure all the necessary related services (speech therapy, physical therapy, or transportation) that you believe your child needs are included. Remember that the school is not obligated to provide any related services that are not written into the IEP.

C. If the school does not agree with you on placement and related services and you are convinced that you are right, *do not sign the IEP.* Ask for the procedural guidelines for mediating a disagreement or for initiating a due process hearing.

D. If you agree on a placement and you are unfamiliar with the teacher, ask about the teacher's qualifications (training and experience) in regard to meeting the special needs of your child.

E. Ensure that your child has *appropriate* opportunities to interact with nonhandicapped children (placement in the least restrictive setting).

VI. Conclusion of the Meeting

A. If the chairperson does not initiate it, ask for a summary of the meeting to review major decisions and follow-up responsibility. Make a written record of this summary.

B. If follow-up responsibility has not been specified, ask who is going to be responsible for each task.

C. Specify what responsibility (teaching objectives or increasing socialization opportunities during after-school hours) you will assume.

D. Ensure that a tentative date is set for reviewing the IEP on at least an annual basis and preferably more frequently.

E. State in what ways and how frequently you would like to communicate with the teacher. Negotiate for these meetings in light of the teachers' preferences.

F. State your desire and intent to work in close cooperation with the school.

G. Express appreciation for the opportunity to share in decision making and for the interest of the school personnel in your child.

A father summed up his feelings about the IEP meeting as follows:

Attending the IEP meeting gave me a psychological boost. I looked around the table and felt very fortunate that every person there really cared that Cindy get a quality education. It made me realize that my wife and I are not alone in our concerns and in our hopes.

All evaluations and IEP conferences do not provide full opportunities for parent involvement. Sometimes they are carried out in far less thorough ways than have been suggested in this chapter. As a parent, you do have the right to participate actively. A helpful strategy to consider is for you to discuss with the professionals in your child's program the way you would prefer to have the evaluation and IEP conference conducted and the type of involvement in the process you would like to have. You can discuss the ideas in this chapter and identify the ones you would particularly like to carry out. The interest you take in the evaluation and in the IEP conference will be evident to the professionals. As stated by one teacher:

Whether we acknowledge it or not, our staff puts a lot more effort into evaluations and IEPs when we know that the parents are going to participate actively. It's motivating for us—it helps us to do our best.

Your interest and involvement can help ensure that evaluations and IEP conferences will lead to a more appropriate education for your child.

Chapter 8

HOW DO YOU GATHER INFORMATION ABOUT PRESCHOOL PROGRAMS IN YOUR COMMUNITY?

Parents looking for a preschool for their handicapped child approach the task in a variety of ways. Some parents strongly rely on the opinions of professionals who know their child and their family, and may even choose a preschool, sight unseen, on the basis of a professional recommendation. One parent made this comment about how a preschool was selected for her son: "They [professionals] were really helpful in placing Paul. They went up there and checked everything out. It took a couple of weeks for all of them to decide where they wanted Paul to go to school."

Other parents may seek professional opinions, but ultimately rely on their own personal observation. A quote from another mother, describing how she found a preschool for her son, best illustrates this contrasting approach: "I saw 15 schools in the area, everything from mainstreaming to private schools—you name it, I visited it. I think that's the only way you can find what you want. You have to go yourself and develop a method."

The approach you take, the resources and information you utilize, and the number of options from which you have to choose depend upon you and your community. The important thing to remember is that your needs and your child's needs should guide your search for a preschool. You are probably more aware of those needs than anyone else is. Thus, the more actively involved you are in deciding upon a preschool, the happier you are likely to be with the choice.

THINKING BACK TO WHAT YOU WANT FROM A PRESCHOOL

If you have read Chapters 2 and 3 of this book, then you have done some thinking about your needs and your child's needs. Take a minute now to look back at Tables 2.4 and 3.2 in Chapters 2 and 3. (If you have not already filled them out, you may want to do so now.) In the last columns in both of these tables is a listing of the things you expect to have provided by a preschool. As a way of putting the information from these two tables into one place so that you can easily look at it, transfer the list of things from Tables 2.4 and 3.2 that you expect from a preschool to Table 8.1.

Think about the items you have listed in Table 8.1 and select the two that you feel are the *most* important (you can designate these with stars or by writing 1. and 2. next to them). Ideally, you will locate a program that can meet *all* of your expectations for a preschool. In the probable event that this does not happen, this list and your thought-out choice of what is of utmost importance can be your guide as you look at the choices around you. The purpose of the remainder of this chapter is to provide you with suggestions about ways you might want to proceed in locating preschool programs in your community.

WHERE TO START AND WHOM TO CALL

Research indicates that friends, relatives, and neighbors are the most common sources of information about preschools for parents of nonhandicapped children. Friends, neighbors, and relatives may not be familiar with services and programs geared for handicapped children. You may want to think about other people and other ways of getting information about appropriate preschools.

Table 8.1. What I expect from a preschool

What I expect for myself	What I expect for my child
1.	1.
2.	2.
3.	3.
4.	4.

Professionals in Your Community

You may want to call the main office of your local school district and ask to speak to the person in charge of special education. Ask this person to describe the preschool services available for handicapped children in the community. Even in states not providing public preschool education to handicapped children, local directors of special education should have information about preschool programs. Other professionals who might have helpful information are elementary special education teachers from your local school system and professionals affiliated with nearby universities, medical centers, infant intervention programs, mental or public health agencies, private clinics, social services, or state education agencies.

In talking to these professionals about preschools, you might want to ask specifically about mainstreamed preschools. Because public preschool typically is not provided to nonhandicapped children, even in states in which it is provided to handicapped children, mainstreaming opportunities are more likely to be available in private preschools than in public ones. Professionals may not think to mention private preschools unless you specifically ask.

Other Parents of Handicapped Young Children

An ideal source of information is other parents whose handicapped children have recently been in preschool or other parents who are themselves trying to locate an appropriate preschool for their child. Parents are a particularly good resource if you are interested in finding out about mainstreamed preschools that are receptive to serving handicapped children. Parent organizations, such as your local Association for Retarded Citizens and the Association for Children with Learning Disabilities, are a starting point for locating parents. The purpose of parent organizations is to provide support and assistance to parents of handicapped children and to work on the development of needed programs. (The resource section contains the name and addresses of the national offices of parent organizations.) The parent of a developmentally delayed child made this comment:

I have found the local ARC chapter (Association for
Retarded Citizens) to be extremely helpful, yet other
parents are reluctant to contact them because they say,
"My child is not 'retarded,' only 'delayed.' " Whatever
you call it, the needs are similar. The ARC has
information and can provide support when you're out
there looking for services.

Printed Materials

Local, state, and private agencies, such as the United Cerebral
Palsy Association, state and local departments of mental health,
local social services agencies, and daycare councils sometimes
develop preschool resource guides for parents. These usually
are not found in bookstores—the trick is laying your hands on
one. The following are strategies for locating these resources:

1. Look in your phone book under the name of your town
   (i.e., "Townville"), your county (i.e., "Jackson County"), or
   your state (i.e., "Kansas"). Read down the list of government departments or agencies and call the one that seems
   closest to what you want.
2. Look in your phone book to see if the various parent organizations listed in the resource section of this book are
   listed. These organizations can help you contact other parents of handicapped children and can provide you with
   information about community resources and programs.
3. Call the nearest hospital and ask for the Social Services
   Office. Describe your child's needs and ask for names, telephone numbers, and locations of doctors, clinics, and out-
   patient services with professionals who may have information that will be helpful to you.
4. Call local universities or community colleges and ask for
   the phone numbers of the Departments of Education, Special Education, or Psychology. Ask to speak with faculty
   members whose interests are in early childhood education,
   preschool education, or special education.

HOW TO ASSESS THIS INFORMATION

In gathering information it is important to remember that the
information each person shares with you is based upon the per-

son's unique experiences, circumstances, and values. It is helpful to talk to a variety of people about the programs in your
community. The next step strictly depends upon your personal
style, your time, and how much you have learned in talking to
various people. It may be that you feel ready to make a decision
based upon the information you have gathered from professionals and/or other parents. It may be that what you have discovered at this point is that options are limited. You may feel
that there is no real choice to be made, that there is only one
clear alternative. If you feel good about this alternative, based
upon information you have gathered, then this may be a logical
stopping point in your search for appropriate preschools. If you
do not feel good about this alternative, you may want to think
about ways to increase preschool options in your community by
working with other parents and professionals interested in early
childhood education. You may also want to continue searching
for other alternatives.

GATHERING MORE INFORMATION

Once you have identified the possible preschool options, the
next step is in making contact with these preschools in order to
continue your assessment. Preliminary information that you can
gather over the telephone or through a brief visit might include
the following:

1. Does the preschool have openings? Is there a waiting list?
2. Is the director of the preschool willing to consider your
   child? (This is particularly important in the case of mainstreamed preschools.)
3. Is there a time when you (and perhaps your child) can
   come for a visit to observe the classroom and to talk with
   staff? Whether or not you take your child with you on this
   first visit depends upon the preschool visited and your
   preference. Some school officials prefer for parents to
   come alone so that they can observe without being dis-
   tracted by their own child. Some school staff may want
   your child to come with you so that you and the staff can
   assess the child's reaction to the group of other children. It
   may be best to arrange two visits: the first being for you to
   observe without your child, and the second being for both
   of you.

4. Does the program have a brochure or any printed information that they can send you?

Gathering preliminary information can eliminate from your consideration schools totally unreceptive to handicapped children. It may be that you will want to make a decision at this point. If not, the next step in deciding among the remaining choices is to gather still more information. The following may be helpful ways to do this:

1. Looking over printed materials, such as brochures or program descriptions, provided to you by the program.
2. Meeting with the staff (director and teacher) of a program.
3. Talking with other parents whose children are enrolled in the program (the director could be asked to supply you with names of parents to call for this information).
4. Visiting the program and seeing what goes on there.

Most parents feel that the only way to really figure out what a program is like is to go see for yourself. Watching how children and teachers work and play together can tell you a lot about the general atmosphere of the preschool. When visiting programs, you will probably want to use your own expectations of what you want from a preschool (Table 8.1) as a guide. In addition to your own specific expectations, the following questions are included to stimulate, not limit or restrict, your investigation of preschool choices. These questions can be used in a way that best suits you. In the final analysis you may rely more on your gut-level reaction and intuition, rather than on facts and figures, in making a decision.

QUESTIONS ABOUT PRESCHOOLS RELATING TO YOUR CHILD'S PROGRESS AND WELL-BEING[24]

Teacher Qualifications

What type of college training does the teacher have?

---

[24] Gold, J.R., and Bergstrom, J.M. *Checking Out Child Care: A Parent Guide.* Day Care and Child Development Council of America, Washington, DC. Some questions in this section were adapted from this guide.

Have the teachers taken special courses related to the education of handicapped children?

Are workshops or training opportunities available for teachers throughout the year?

How do the teachers feel about their ability to teach handicapped children?

Teacher's Interactions with Children

Does the teacher smile and look directly at the children when talking with them?

Does the teacher appear to be physically relaxed with the children when touching, talking with, and approaching them?

Do the children appear to trust the teacher and freely turn to him or her for help, information, and comfort?

Is the teacher skilled at communicating with nonverbal children? Does he or she know sign language? Is the teacher sensitive to nonverbal cues, such as gestures, facial expressions, and postures?

Where does the teacher appear to spend most of his or her time—working with children, arranging materials, or talking with other adults, parents, or staffmembers?

Does the teacher display humor and common sense in dealing with children?

Does the teacher seem to be easily hassled if things are not going right?

How does the teacher reward and discipline a child? Do you feel comfortable with these methods?

Is the teacher's talk with the children heavily sprinkled with do's and don'ts?

Teacher's Attitudes toward Individual Needs

Do the teacher's expectations and treatments differ for girls and for boys?

Has the teacher had experience with handicapped children in the classroom or elsewhere? Did these handicapped children have special needs similar to those of your child?

Does the teacher's attitude and that of the preschool reflect (through the selection of pictures, photographs, and books) an awareness of, and respect for, ethnic and cultural backgrounds?

Does the teacher categorize children?

How does the teacher describe his or her approach to meeting the individual needs of each child? Do you think the teacher will be able to meet your child's needs?

Individualized Instruction

How many children are in the class? How many instructors? (Instructors might include teacher aides, parent volunteers, or older students.)

Does the number of children compared to the number of instructors seem to be reasonable?

Are children grouped for instruction according to skill level or chronological age? Are groupings flexible?

Are special materials and equipment available for children with handicaps (e.g., prone standers, corner chairs, braille readers, or books in large print)?

Do children's needs in different skill areas seem to be taken into consideration?

The Arrangement of Space in the Preschool

Is there enough space for the number of children? Is it divided? Is there an outdoor play area?

If space is divided, who goes where? Is the division made by age, sex, interest, or type of handicap? Are there small areas where a child can go to be alone?

Are furniture and equipment arranged in such a manner that your child can crawl, walk, or navigate in a wheelchair?

Are there spaces for children to work or play quietly and actively with materials and equipment?

Are there adequate areas and facilities for children to rest and sleep?

Are there special areas for a variety of activities: blocks, reading, dress-up, or arts and crafts? Are the potentially noisy and active areas—blocks, jungle gyms, and the housekeeping center—separated physically from the quiet areas—books, puzzles, and art centers?

Are there areas where specialists (e.g., speech therapist, or physical therapist) can work with children and teachers?

Is the preschool building, including bathrooms and playground, accessible to children with mobility impairments?

Related Support Services

Are the related services (e.g., speech therapy, physical therapy, occupational therapy, mobility and orientation training, audiological services, counseling, and health services) needed by your child currently available?

How frequently and for what period of time are related services available?

Who provides the related services? What is the relationship between the teacher and related-service providers?

Are services offered individually or in small groups?

Is the teacher willing to follow up in the classroom on recommendations from related-service providers?

Is funding for related services a certainty?

If related services are not currently part of program, does the staff know how to find and use community resources?

Emotional and Social Climate of the Preschool

Who is the primary population being served? (Observe the classroom and get to know the characteristics of the children currently enrolled.)

Do the children appear to be comfortable and free with other children in the group, or are there numerous fights and disturbances?

Do the children encourage one another, appear to play well with others in the group, and work cooperatively among themselves? Do they do things without constant interference from adults?

Does the teacher help to mediate potentially explosive situations, such as fights over toys, name-calling, or physical aggressiveness?

Do opportunities exist for handicapped children to interact with nonhandicapped children in the classroom? Do such opportunities exist outside the classroom?

How do handicapped children in the program interact with each other?

Does the program provide opportunities for the children to experience risks—physical and emotional? Is the program overly protective and specialized for your child?

Do teachers encourage independence, e.g., are children permitted to test their physical abilities and to master difficult tasks with teacher supervision?

Are children encouraged to work independently without teacher attention or reinforcement for some parts of the day?

Keeping Track of the Child's Progress and Development

Are children assessed in all developmental areas, such as speech and language, social, emotional, and physical development?

Are annual goals and short-term objectives formulated in all developmental areas?

How frequently is the progress of the child monitored? How frequently and in what way is this information shared with parents?

Are parents involved in helping to plan the child's educational program?

QUESTIONS ABOUT PRESCHOOLS RELATING TO YOUR OWN NEEDS

Each of the categories of parent needs identified in this section is discussed in depth in Chapter 3. Again, you need to think about what your family's priorities are and what your expectations are for how the preschool can meet those needs. These priorities and expectations can be translated into questions for you to explore when you visit preschools.

Professional Involvement So Parents Can Relax

Can parents trust teachers to do a good job teaching the child? (This will have to develop over time, but do the basic elements of trust seem to be present?)

Frequent Contacts with Teachers

Are teachers willing to engage in frequent interactions with parents?

Are opportunities available for you and the teachers to have frequent interactions (e.g., at drop-off or pick-up times)?

Do teachers seem to be willing to listen to what you have to say (including feelings of frustration, resentment, inadequacy, or anger) in an open, nondefensive, and nonjudgmental manner?

Are parents able to observe the classroom?

Parent Counseling

Do staffmembers provide counseling, or is this service provided through other community resources?

Parent Training

Does the program provide opportunities for improving parent-child interaction (e.g., workshops to increase parents' knowledge and skills or opportunities to observe staffmembers and learn educational techniques from them)?

Program Participation

Does the program provide opportunities for parent participation (e.g., advisory board membership and decision-making opportunities or opportunities to volunteer as an aide in the classroom or with a special project outside of the classroom)?

Are participation opportunities available for all family members (e.g., fathers, siblings, or grandparents)?

Contacts with Other Parents

Are structured opportunities available to meet with other parents who may share your feelings, perspectives, and needs (e.g., parent support groups or potluck dinners)?

Are unstructured opportunities to meet with parents available (e.g., drop-off and pick-up arrangements that encourage parent interaction or having a quiet place with a coffee pot and a parent bulletin board)?

Cost of Program

What is the cost of the program? (The local school system is financially responsible if educational services for handi-

capped children aged 3–5 are legally mandated in your state.)
When are tuition payments due?
Are scholarships available?

Convenience of Program

How far is the program from your home?
Are parent carpools encouraged, supported, or available?
Does the preschool provide bus service? What is the cost?

Is Daycare Provided?

What are the preschool's hours of operation?
Is a full-day program an option?
Are other parents interested in organizing a full-day program if
    one is not available? Are there other parents willing to keep
    your child in their home during the hours that school is out
    while you are at work?
Are afternoon daycare programs available nearby and could you
    or someone else transport your child to these programs?
Does the preschool have a summer school program available?
    What are the goals and purposes of this program?

It should be pointed out again that the single most important thing to assess when you visit a preschool is the teachers'
receptiveness and flexibility in attending to your family's unique
situation.

MAKING THE DECISION

Three things are necessary to consider when making a decision.
The first is that the facts and figures may tell you one thing and
your gut reaction (intuitive feelings) may indicate another.
Sometimes further reflection on a decision will help you to
understand why the two are out of line. Perhaps a very important need, which you had not identified before, is influencing
your feelings. It is important to pay attention to your feelings. If
this is happening, take some more time to think about the decision before committing yourself.

The second consideration is that a decision does not have
to be etched in stone. If the program for your child does not

Table 8.2. Decision checklist

Preschool options	Child needs			Parent needs		
	Adaptive physical facilities	Interaction with normal peers	Warm and accepting teachers	Professional involvement so parents can relax	Frequent contacts with staff	Chance to meet other parents of handicapped children
1. Private main-streamed preschool sponsored by neighborhood church	no	yes	no	maybe	maybe	no
2. Developmental center, subsidized by local education agency	yes	no	yes	yes	yes	yes
3. Private main-streamed preschool with director who is a special educator	yes	yes	yes	yes	yes	maybe

work out for some reason, you always have the option of making a change. Helen Harrison[25] makes this comment:

When parents of a handicapped child switch specialists and look for new opinions, doctors call it "shopping around." They disapprove of it. But it was through shopping around that we finally discovered the small dayschool where Ed is now making excellent progress.

The third consideration is that there may be ways you can make improvements in what the program can offer your child. The father of a blind child described the way he and his wife devised an education program for their child in a state without mandated preschool services. They placed their child in a private, mainstreamed preschool with a small teacher/pupil ratio and a teacher who they thought was especially gifted and interested in working with handicapped children. Because this teacher was certified, they were able to get a student teacher from a local university to do her field placement at the preschool. They could not afford to pay an occupational therapist to work with their child on a regular basis, but they were able to hire this specialist to train the student teacher to work with their child and to do periodic supervision and evaluation. Through their ingenuity, they were able to pull together many resources without having to bankrupt themselves in the process. They felt that the preschool teacher, the student teacher, the other preschool children, their child, and their family all benefited from the program that developed.

Once you have gathered the information you feel that you need on each preschool option, then the time has come to tie together the needs you identified in Chapters 2 and 3 with information on preschools in your community. A decision checklist is provided to help you to do this. Table 8.2 is a decision checklist that has been filled out for illustrative purposes. A blank checklist has been provided for you to fill out based on your own needs and your child's needs (Table 8.3).

---

[25] Harrison, H. 1983. *The Premature Baby Book: A Parents' Guide to Coping and Caring in the First Years.* St. Martin's Press, New York.

DIRECTIONS FOR USING
THE DECISION CHECKLIST

1. List each preschool option that you are considering in the left column.

2. List the top three or four child needs that you expect a preschool program to meet, as summarized in Table 8.1.

3. List the top three or four family needs that you expect a preschool program to meet, as summarized in Table 8.1.

4. Think about each preschool option separately in terms of its ability to meet each child need and family need. Mark a "yes," "no," or "maybe" under each need, according to the extent you feel the preschool can meet this need.

5. In addition, you may want to write down your general impressions of each preschool.

Once you have developed your own decision checklist, you should be better prepared to make the appropriate preschool choice for yourself and for your child.

Table 8.3. Decision checklist

Preschool option	Child needs	Parent needs
1.		
2.		
3.		

HOW CAN YOU BEST PREPARE YOUR CHILD AND YOURSELF FOR THE NEW PRESCHOOL?

Looking back over their child's initial entry into preschool, parents we have interviewed recalled a lot of things they wish they had done. Chapter 9 contains some of their suggestions, as well as our own, about how to prepare your child for this new experience. Some level of preparation is usually necessary, whether your child will be attending a mainstreamed or a specialized setting. The issues and levels of preparation may differ according to your own interest and time availability, and according to the developmental needs of your child. For example, if your child is severely handicapped and entering a mainstreamed setting for the first time, you and your child's teacher may need to do extensive preparation activities with the nonhandicapped children in the classroom. On the other hand, if your child, who is mildly developmentally delayed and has cerebral palsy, has been attending a specialized day program and will now enter a similar specialized preschool program, your preparation should involve much less time.

In addition, you may have feelings, worries, or concerns related to the fact that your child will be entering a new school program, perhaps for the first time. In Chapter 10 the focus is on parental concerns, and guidelines and suggestions are offered for addressing these concerns.

The chapters in this section are particularly important for you if the preschool is your child's first experience in a program of any kind. If it is, you may feel what we call *transition effects* —some stressful moments in settling your child into a new school environment. This section is geared primarily toward what you can do at home to prepare for the preschool experience. Also, because a smooth transition depends on adequate planning and communication between you and the preschool staff, some suggestions for building an open, comfortable parent-teacher relationship are included.

Chapter 9

HOW CAN YOU PREPARE YOUR CHILD FOR THE NEW PRESCHOOL?

Starting something new is always easier, and can be more fun, if you are well prepared. All children entering a new preschool program make a number of major adjustments: to the new teachers (who at first will probably appear as "strange adults"); to a new group of children; to the concept of schedules or planned activities; and to the expectations suddenly placed upon them to perform, to get along with others, or to be somewhat independent. When a child has special needs, these adjustments may be harder. In addition, the teachers as well as the other children (whether or not they are handicapped) need to make adjustments to the new preschool members. The purpose of this chapter is to help you prepare your child for entering the new preschool. In doing so, some guidelines are provided that we hope will make this preparation easier for you and for your child.

It is important to remember that guidelines or suggestions cannot possibly be appropriate for everyone; please select those that best apply to you and to your child. For example, many of you will be considering a preschool in a specialized rather than in a mainstreamed setting. In that case, you may find our suggestions for fostering positive relationships between handicapped and nonhandicapped preschoolers less helpful. Some of these suggestions, however, may apply to other settings, such as the interactions of your handicapped child with peers in your neighborhood or in your church or synagogue.

GENERAL GUIDELINES

The following list contains several things you might do in preparation for sending your child to preschool:

1. Orient your child to the preschool environment and activities.
2. Let your child know the general expectations of the preschool.
3. Help the teacher learn how to handle your child's special needs.
4. Help prepare your child for interacting with nonhandicapped children (if your child enters a mainstreamed preschool).
5. Help prepare your child for interacting with other handicapped children.
6. Discuss with the teacher whether a need exists to prepare nonhandicapped classmates for interacting with your child.

The rest of this chapter provides suggestions for carrying out each of these guidelines.

Orienting Your Child to the New Preschool

For children as well as adults, providing information in advance is a good way to eliminate anxiety about a new experience. Your child should be familiar with the general preschool environment and with the typical preschool day of activities. Two ways to accomplish this are: 1) talk to your child's teacher about the preschool routines and then explain these to your child, and 2) take your child for a visit to the school. While you are describing the preschool, encourage your child to ask questions about things that may be of concern:

1. Is the teacher nice?
2. What are the other kids like?
3. What kinds of toys will they have?
4. What do they serve for lunch?

Of course, any discussion you have with your child must be adapted to his or her level of communication and understanding. If your child has major communication delays, you will not be able to have such a discussion. However, you can still introduce your child to a typical preschool day by learning about the preschool routine from the teacher and then trying out the routine at home. For example, see if you can introduce several structured activities from the preschool routine at home, such as water play, coloring, and simple dressing skills. You may want to set up regular times for these activities consistent with the schedule at preschool. Another suggestion is to try to anticipate the aspects of the new preschool that might feel strange or intimidating to your child. Some children may be frightened by the noise and hubbub accompanying most preschool activities; if possible, take your child to a local playground, to story hours at the library, or to church-sponsored activities to familiarize him or her to new, lively settings. Most typical preschool days include both noisy and quiet times. You can introduce both types of environments and reward your child for demonstrating the appropriate type of behavior in each situation. Going from a noisy playground to the children's room in the public library may be one way to demonstrate contrasting environments.

Regardless of the severity of your preschooler's handicap or level of ability, a visit to the preschool may say more than a thousand words. Your child will be able to observe the actual toys and activities that are available and, in some cases, may think of other things to ask about. You may even want to invite the preschool teacher to visit your home, so that your child can be introduced in a familiar, secure setting. This could be particularly helpful if your preschooler is more severely handicapped and you're not sure how much the child observes or understands on a visit to the preschool. It is important that your child feel comfortable with the new preschool teacher. If you believe such a visit would be appropriate in your situation, you might want to plan in advance special things your child could share with the teacher, such as a favorite record, blanket, or toy.

You may want to consider introducing your child to the new preschool gradually. For example, it may be beneficial to make several visits to the preschool prior to actual enrollment, which would allow your child to become familiar with a whole host of new activities. For young children who have had no prior preschool or daycare experience, a gradual introduction will probably be less anxiety provoking. One mother described her own situation:

Karen started preschool when she was three. Until that time, she and I were together every day, almost all the time. It was a big adjustment for both of us to learn to be apart. In many ways, I was probably the one who had the most problems. Anyway, when the time came for her to start, Karen went for one hour per day for the first week, and two hours per day for the second week. It was not until the third week that she attended the whole morning session of the preschool. I think this arrangement helped both of us. I have recommended it to many other parents.

Let Your Child Know the Preschool's Expectations

At some point prior to enrollment you should review the preschool schedule and routine with your child, and explain the type of things that will be expected. For example, some preschools have a requirement that children be able to use the toilet properly on their own. Your child needs to know this. If your child is not toilet trained and is prone to wetting pants, he or she will need to know how that situation will be handled. Again, if your child has substantial cognitive and language delays, you will not be able to explain sufficiently what will be expected of the child. Instead, as one parent recommended, you could try to imitate aspects of the preschool routine at home.

After you have identified some of the expectations and demands that may be placed on your child, you might want to adapt your home environment to be consistent with as many aspects of the preschool environment as possible. For example, you might want to work on improving your child's attention span, ability to follow directions, or ability to sit in a chair throughout the duration of an activity. After visiting the preschool, if you observe that the children usually sit in a chair at a table to color or to play, and your child always plays on the floor, you might want to initiate some table games or activities at home. Often preschools have "rug-time," during which children are expected to sit or lie on their rug and to work quietly or independently. You can prepare your child for meeting this demand at home by practicing rug-time.

If your child has behavior that you think will present problems for him or her or for the teachers in the new setting, ask the teachers about this. Ask them how they will handle these behaviors in the classroom. If you think the techniques they plan to use are good ones and could be used at home, try them before the school year begins.

When your child begins preschool, the teacher will probably work with you on eliminating any specific behavior problems (such as temper tantrums, shouting, or bothering other children) and on introducing necessary self-help skills. However, if you feel that your child needs to acquire certain skills before entering preschool, and if you are interested in working on such skills with your child at home, talking to the teacher prior to the start of school about the techniques used at school would provide you with direction for working with your child. In addition, you may want to order some of the parent training manuals cited in the resources section under "Parental Support."

Prepare the Teacher for Handling Your Child's Unique Needs

Most teachers like to have information in advance about their prospective students. The kinds of information particularly helpful to teachers include the following: your child's favorite activities, the types of discipline you have found to be successful, specific hints about what your child finds rewarding, how to position or handle your child if he or she is physically handicapped, how to communicate with a nonverbal child, how to handle any adaptive equipment (e.g., wheelchair, braces, or hearing aid); how to respond to a seizure; and what special instructional materials, such as large-print books for a visually impaired child, are appropriate. This additional information is likely to increase both the teacher's confidence in working with your child and the consistency of approach between home and school.

There are several procedures you could use to inform the teacher about your child's handicap and special needs. If you completed the table of your child's needs in Chapter 2, bring it to the school and review it with the teacher. Using the table, you will be able to show the teacher how you plan to meet your child's various social and educational needs, both within and outside the preschool setting. For example, the teacher may find it helpful to know that while she is working on increasing social interactions and language development in the school setting, you are also taking your child to a speech therapist once a week and to a mainstreamed swimming program on weekends. If your child's preschool prepares IEPs, you should share such information with the teacher during the IEP meeting. If IEP meetings are not held, you might consider arranging a collaborative conference between the preschool staff and any specialists working with your child. Such a conference is a good way of sharing important information and designating who will be working on each skill area.

You will make the teacher's job a lot easier if you see to it that all relevant records on your child are available. In addition, many teachers would be eager to know about resource persons, such as doctors or psychologists, with whom you have worked and whom they would call if questions should arise. You may feel comfortable serving as such a resource person; if so, let the teacher know how, when, and where he or she can get in touch with you.

Help To Prepare Your Child for Interacting with Nonhandicapped Peers

If you have already decided to send your handicapped preschooler to a regular preschool, you are probably aware of the many social benefits of mainstreaming at the early childhood level. For example, research has shown that language, play, and socialization skills of mild, moderately, and severely handicapped preschoolers can improve as a result of interactions with nonhandicapped preschoolers. In addition to modeling or demonstrating certain behaviors, nonhandicapped children may be able to teach certain skills to your child. One mother of a child with cerebral palsy, who attended a mainstreamed preschool, told us:

My husband and I can't exactly go out and get on
Charles's little tricycle and show him how to ride it, but
at school they have a trike. Once he saw all of the other
kids riding it, then he started trying to learn. You should
see him ride it now.

Various developmentally challenging skills, such as climbing a jungle gym or using other playground equipment, can be learned by your child in a similar fashion. The important thing to do is to encourage your child to interact with the nonhandicapped children in a mainstreamed setting. Both you and the teacher may need to demonstrate and guide your child through such interactions in order to ensure that they occur.

An important role for you is to help your child build friendships with these other children. One parent describes the strategy she used when her family moved from one community to another:

I had real fears about John having to enter a new
preschool in the middle of the year. It seemed that his
visual impairment was enough of a disadvantage
without him also having to be the new kid on the block.
My husband had an idea that turned out very well.
Before we moved, we located a preschool in the new
community. It came very highly recommended to us. My
husband and I visited the program and met the teacher
during the hectic weekend of buying a house. When we
returned home, we started a pen-pal program with the
youngsters who would soon be John's classmates. We
sent them a picture of John and some of his artwork. We
also had John dictate some sentences about what he
likes to do. We wrote the sentences for him. The teacher
was delighted over the idea and sent us back a tape of
the children singing. At the end of the songs, they all
said a few words on the tape welcoming John. When we
finally moved, John already felt friendships had
been made.

Another strategy for you to consider is to meet a couple of the nonhandicapped preschoolers in advance and invite them over to your house to meet and to play with your child. Help your child learn to answer the questions that might be encountered: "Why are you in a wheelchair? Why do you talk funny? Why can't you walk and run?"

The mother of a child with spina bifida describes the importance of her daughter being able to talk about her handicap with the other children in her classroom:

Sally's back has scars on it. I've seen children look at it and ask their mothers, "What's wrong with her back?" The mothers usually say, "I don't know." I think that leaves the child with much worse thoughts in mind than the reality of what's wrong with Sally's back. So Sally is now able to tell people about her back herself. She now explains to anyone that asks that she had surgery, and that's why her back is scarred.

The best way for your child to handle questions and even teasing (an unfortunate but possible situation) is to learn to stand up for himself or herself. This is a difficult skill to teach nonhandicapped adults, let alone handicapped preschoolers. However, if your child does complain to you about being teased, or asks you why he or she is called "slow-poke," or other names, here are a few responses you might try. You can assure your child that he or she is lovable by demonstrating your own love to the child. You can try to explain that some children are slower or less able to do certain tasks than others, just as some are fatter or thinner than others. You can explain that some children may say things that they shouldn't and may call other children names, and that those children should be ignored. Although learning to stand up for oneself takes time and maturity, this can still begin during the preschool years.

Jane Schulz,[26] the mother of a mentally retarded son, who is now an adult, offers sound advice about learning to stand up for oneself early:

---

[26] Schulz, J. 1979. Facing the label. *Education Unlimited*, 1(4):50–53.

*The strongest example I can present is the experience of
my son, who is mentally retarded. Although aware of his
retardation, he was raised and educated in protective
environments; he was never called "stupid," "fat," or
"dumb." When he went to work he failed, not because he
lacked the necessary skills, but because he had not
learned to deal with the threats and jeers of his
coworkers.*

Finally, your child may even be able to increase participation with nonhandicapped children if games and activities are adapted to meet the child's own needs. This can be done by teaching your child modified versions of typical preschool games at home. If you visit the preschool or talk to the teacher prior to your child's enrollment, you may learn what some of these games and activities are. You can try them at home with your child and with any other siblings, and make adaptations or equipment substitutions if needed. You may want to suggest that the preschool purchase the special equipment that your child needs, such as a larger or softer ball. If no preschool funds are available, an alternative is to let your child take special equipment from home to play with at school.

Help To Prepare Your Child for Interacting with Handicapped Peers

It is important to make your own child aware of other types of handicapping conditions. Providing such information can help the child recognize the fact that everyone has strengths and limitations, and can also help your child identify his or her own strengths and weaknesses. Visits to specialized daycare centers or preschools for handicapped children can introduce your child to a range of disabilities. By talking to a teacher or to the center director beforehand, you might be able to arrange for your child to meet several of the children. Discuss the strengths of different children, being careful not to overlook the handicap itself. Here is how one mother explained to her daughter, Susie, who had spina bifida and who was confined to a wheelchair, about Donald, a hearing-impaired boy who wore a hearing aid and used sign language as he spoke:

Mother: Donald wears a special box and a special plug in his ear to help him hear. You use a wheelchair to help you get around. See, you both have something special to use every day!

Susie: If Donald uses my chair will he get around better?

Mother: No, because he can use his own legs. Remember how he could run across the playground and play on the swings?

But you don't need any help hearing—maybe Donald can help you on the playground and you can learn to talk to Donald with your hands!

Very often teachers take the time to introduce children in the above manner, but there will be opportunities when you might want to try it. When you are preparing your child for interacting with other children who have special needs, encourage him or her to think of ways to help these children. There are also many storybooks, films, and television shows available that feature handicapped characters, several of which are mentioned in the resources section under the heading "Media and Children's Books." If possible, introduce your child to such books or shows, and discuss different types of handicaps and how they are portrayed.

Help To Prepare Nonhandicapped Children for Interacting with Handicapped Peers

One reaction that some children have to other children who are noticeably handicapped is fear that they may "catch" whatever the handicapped child has. A mother of a handicapped child describes how her daughter's teachers handled this situation:

One day at the beginning of the school year, a little boy in Carol's class started crying, because he didn't want to play with Carol. When the teacher asked him why, he said he was afraid he would have to be in a wheelchair like Carol if he played with her. This opened up a discussion with the entire class about handicaps, about Carol's handicap, and about how differences like that are not contagious and are not caused by germs. Then

the teacher let all of the children get in Carol's
wheelchair. That little boy and Carol became very good
friends over the year. I think the teachers did a great job
with helping the class adjust to Carol. By talking openly
about things, everyone's fears could be aired and
handled.

Other ways in which teachers can provide information on handicapping conditions to all the preschool children include puppet shows, stories, books about handicaps, or question-and-answer sessions, some of which are listed in the resources section. Many preschools have successfully used handicapped dolls (e.g., dolls with a leg brace, a hearing aid, or thick glasses) during free play time as a way to familiarize children with individual differences.

The teacher might develop curriculum units on various types of handicaps, which may include role-taking and simulation activities. For example, children could take turns being "handicapped" (e.g., wearing a blindfold or using crutches) for a part of the day, in order to develop some sensitivity toward, and awareness of, handicapping conditions. By introducing peer tutoring (in which one child instructs another in a specific skill) and small group sessions (in which handicapped and nonhandicapped children work together), the teacher can help promote social interactions.

ADJUSTMENT PERIOD

The goal of all this preparation is for your child to experience a smooth transition into the new preschool. Although you may be expecting this to be the case, it is usually wise to anticipate adjustment problems that could occur, particularly if your child is going to be in a mainstreamed setting for the first time. Interviews with parents have indicated that many handicapped children entering a mainstreamed preschool do go through a definite period of adjustment. Parents describe this period as difficult—sometimes marked by teasing, stares, or questioning by the nonhandicapped children. However, these parents say that this adjustment period had a very positive outcome: preparing their child for the real world. If by now you feel that your child might indeed experience a difficult adjustment phase, you might want to develop a plan for identifying and handling such problems. One strategy would be to schedule a regular meeting with your child's teacher for the first several months, perhaps on a biweekly basis. This will enable you and the teacher to discuss any problems and to intervene early if your child needs special help.

Chapter 10

HOW CAN YOU PREPARE YOURSELF FOR THE NEW PRESCHOOL?

Parents, like their children, need to make certain adjustments to the new preschool. For example, many parents experience difficulty separating from their child for the first time (especially when the child cries or becomes anxious). One mother shares her own experience as follows:

I dread taking Kim to preschool. She starts to cry when we turn into the preschool parking lot. By the time I stop the car, she is clinging to me like a vine. When I finally get her inside, my stomach is cramped and my heart is racing. The teacher assures me that she is fine within five minutes after the time I leave. Kim soon forgets she was upset, but sometimes I feel tied up in knots for the rest of the day.

Parents of handicapped children in particular may feel the need to make certain emotional adjustments when their child enters preschool. Whether or not their child is handicapped, some parents spend a large part of their day with their child and may thus find the separation imposed by the preschool program difficult. Other parents may welcome the separation, because they will have more time for themselves and for their other responsibilities.

Parents also need to adjust to the preschool teacher's style and to develop trust in the teacher's judgment and abilities. A theme repeated in our interviews with parents of handicapped preschoolers was the importance parents placed on teacher competencies. The abilities of teachers were perceived as important, not only in increasing child progress but also in helping parents to relax and to enjoy a break from the daily care of their child.

Often it is difficult for parents to observe their handicapped child participating in activities with a larger group of peers for the first time. This difficulty may be even more pronounced if the peer group includes nonhandicapped children. The mother of a 4-year-old Down's syndrome youngster in a mainstreamed classroom shares her experiences: "I thought Larry was doing so well learning his "m" sounds and all, until I watched him playing with all those nonhandicapped children! His language delay suddenly seemed so obvious!"

The nature and degree of adjustment to the above situations depends largely on the individual needs of parents and on the type of preschool setting in which their child is enrolled. The purpose of this chapter is to present guidelines and ideas to assist you in preparing yourself for the new preschool experience.

GENERAL GUIDELINES

The following guidelines might be useful for preparing yourself for a positive preschool experience:

1. Aim toward a positive and open relationship with teachers.
2. Aim toward a positive and open relationship with other parents.
3. Prepare yourself for dealing with adjustment problems that your child might have.
4. Learn to coordinate and monitor the services that are available to you and your child.

These guidelines are based on suggestions made by other parents of preschool children. Your own need for preparation may depend upon various considerations: whether or not your other children (if you have any) attended preschool; whether your handicapped child will be attending preschool in a mainstreamed or in a specialized setting; and what suits your own personality and needs.

Aiming toward a Positive and Open Relationship with Teachers

The type of relationship that you will ultimately have with your child's teacher depends on a combination of factors. Ideally, you will have a parent-teacher relationship characterized by respect and openness. There are things teachers can do to foster positive relationships with parents, such as working on positive attitudes toward parent involvement, developing friendly, open communication styles, and sharing instructional knowledge and programming. In teacher training programs greater emphasis is currently being placed on working with parents. For now, what kinds of things can you do to prepare yourself for an equal, open, and satisfying relationship with your child's teacher?

In earlier research with parents of handicapped preschoolers, we learned that parents placed a high value on developing informal relationships with teachers. "Informal" meant that they could talk freely and openly about their child's program, progress, or problems at any time—in the school parking lot or on the playground, as well as during organized parent conferences. This type of contact allowed parents to have a give-and-take relationship with the teachers. As one parent comments:

I really value being able to check-in with the teacher when I pick up Roger. She'll often tell me about something clever he said or about whether he was particularly lively or flat in his interactions with others. I have developed trust in Mrs. Whelan [the teacher] because she tells me both about Roger's successes and about his problems. One day she told me that he cried for about 30 minutes and seemed very blue. She told me that the aide in the classroom took him into another room and just held him. I was so glad that she alerted me to his sadness, and also I was reassured to know that expressing feelings in the classroom is handled in a nurturing way.

Establishing this type of comfortable relationship with your child's teacher will probably make it easier to share your ideas on your child's educational program and to obtain information about your child's progress. It is also important for you to be able to share your needs with your child's teacher. If you have trouble identifying or expressing these needs, you may want to refer to the exercise and chart you completed in Chapter 3. (If you have not yet read Chapter 3, you might find it helpful to do so now.) Think about the different needs you may have (e.g., the need to be involved in your child's program; the need for carpool arrangements and full-time daycare, because you work; and the need for training in certain skills for working with your child) and how you would most prefer these needs to be met. It is unlikely that teachers will be able to guess each parent's needs correctly. It is important for you to tell them yours. For example, you may have certain preferences:

—Even though many parents prefer making informal, frequent contact with the teacher or receiving a quick progress report when they pick up their child at the end of the day, you prefer talking in a less hurried, quiet setting. Let the teacher know your preference early so that the two of you can arrange specific times for meeting.

—Although you enjoy pot-luck dinners with other parents and opportunities for parent involvement at the preschool, what you really want is some training in special techniques to use with your child at home. If you make your child's teacher aware of this preference, he or she may help locate specific activities or programs for you to try.

—You may feel very uncomfortable watching your child interacting in a large group of peers. The child may seem left out, or perhaps seem more handicapped because of a higher level of functioning of the other children; this may particularly be true if your child attends a mainstreamed preschool. In any event, if you communicate your uneasiness to the teacher, he or she may be able to help you to interpret your observations and be supportive of your feelings.

Developing a Positive and Open Relationship with Other Parents

Parents of the children enrolled in a preschool all share a common experience: observing and participating in the education and development of their children. This experience usually lasts for at least one year, and during that time it is likely that friendships with other parents will develop. Such friendships may serve a purely social function, but they may also become a valuable source of emotional and psychological support for you. A mother relates her own experience:

Sometimes I became friends with certain other moms because our two little ones were buddies. But that wasn't always the case; at times it seemed that my making friends with other mothers helped our kids get to know each other. It didn't matter, though. I needed to be able to talk to other parents; it became my *need, not Larry's [her son].*

If your child attends a mainstreamed program, you should keep in mind that parents of the nonhandicapped children may be unsure of how to relate to parents of handicapped children. Sometimes parents of handicapped children can set an example:

Peter's parents set the pattern by accepting and acknowledging the fact that their child was handicapped but was not to be pitied. Because they seemed to accept the reality so fully, those around them, like myself, accepted it and went on from there. I never forgot that Peter was handicapped, but the fact faded into the background. Because his parents were open, were willing to answer questions, and were eager to have Peter participate in the classroom, I accepted him and seldom gave a second thought to the fact that Peter was handicapped.[27]

---

[27] Eisinger, L. 1983. Peter in the classroom: Another parent's view. In: T. Dougan, L. Isbell, and P. Vyas (eds.), *We Have Been There: A Guidebook for Parents of People with Mental Retardation.* Abingdon Press, Nashville, TN.

In earlier work with parents of preschoolers, we investigated what kinds of parent-to-parent interactions took place in a large, preschool mainstreaming setting. Parents of the handicapped preschoolers reported that they tend to interact equally with other parents of handicapped preschoolers and with parents of nonhandicapped preschoolers. Such interactions included activities like pot-luck dinners, parent meetings, or phone calls. On the other hand, most parents of nonhandicapped preschoolers indicated that they would be more likely to interact with other parents of nonhandicapped children. Of course, many factors influence such interactions, not the least of which are things like outside interests, where one lives, and with whom one's child plays. Nonetheless, it may be that parents of nonhandicapped children could benefit from some information and communication about handicapping conditions. One parent told us:

Being with all those other parents made us like an international pot-luck! There were black, white, Indian, and Asian parents of cerebral palsied, visually impaired, hearing impaired, mentally retarded, and nonhandicapped children all swapping stories about their kids!

An informal parent meeting can be a good ice-breaker for parents, providing an opportunity to make introductions or to learn a little about each other's children. If your child is in a mainstreamed setting, the initial parent meeting is an ideal time for the teacher to present the concept of mainstreaming and to promote discussion of some of the issues involved. The discussion of mainstreaming should include how it is being implemented and, specifically, how the staff, children, and parents can support the needs of the handicapped and of the nonhandicapped children. Often, as the parents of the nonhandicapped children learn about the various types of handicaps and the strengths as well as the weaknesses that many handicapped preschoolers do have, they become even more supportive of the concept of mainstreaming. The parents of a visually impaired child describe how an orientation meeting for parents held during the spring, before preschool began in the fall, helped smooth the way for their child's mainstreaming experience:

*During the orientation meeting the teacher told the
group of parents that there would be a visually impaired
child in the school, and that we, as his mother and
father, would be happy to answer any questions about
things they might want to know. One or two said a little
something, but they didn't really open up then. The
teacher told us later that when she made home visits
over the summer, every one of the parents mentioned it
during the visit. She said none of them seemed
particularly worried once she assured them that she felt
comfortable teaching David. What was good about the
way things were handled was that everyone had from
May until August to think about how they felt and to
talk to their children about it.*

A later parent meeting, after parents get to know each
other, may be an appropriate time to discuss parental concerns
about mainstreaming. It is important that parents of handicapped children be prepared for such a discussion by thinking
in advance about what they want to say and by anticipating their
likely reactions to the comments of other parents. One mother
suggested that all parents of handicapped children get together
to discuss their concerns or fears about preschool mainstreaming before the larger group meeting. With careful teacher or
group-leader direction, such a discussion between parents of
handicapped and nonhandicapped children can result in everyone feeling more positive about the mainstreaming experience.
The following comment by Pat Vyas,[28] mother of a Down's syndrome child, attests to the fact that preschool mainstreaming
has something to offer to other parents of nonhandicapped children as well:

*Our class is a co-op, and the parents share in the work of
running the class and the school. I know that some of
the other parents have reservations about Peter's being
in the class with their child, and also about working
with him there. But I think that the experience of*

---

[28] Vyas, P. 1983. Just another little kid. In: T. Dougan, L. Isbell, and P. Vyas (eds.),
*We Have Been There: A Guidebook for Parents of People with Mental Retarda-
tion.* Abingdon Press, Nashville, TN.

*working with a Down's syndrome child has been a
positive one for them.*

Aside from providing information, parent meetings and
other types of parent involvement activities may be aimed at
increasing interaction among parents. One strategy that some
preschools use to help build relationships is to have a buddy
system for parents who have children with similar needs. For
example, two or three parents who each have a preschooler
with cerebral palsy might enjoy sharing anecdotes about day-
to-day challenges or information on special resources or archi-
tectural modifications for the home.

Anticipating Some Adjustment Problems

The Boy Scout motto, "Be prepared," is probably the best single
bit of advice for minimizing adjustment problems. What can you
do to ensure that *you* will "be prepared?" First, talk with other
parents whose children have attended the preschool. Find out
how well their child, handicapped or nonhandicapped, adjusted
to the program. If there were any problems, also try to learn
what, if anything, parents, teachers, or children themselves did
to bring about a positive outcome. Second, if you are so inclined, work toward establishing a parent support group to deal
with special issues and concerns that might arise throughout
the course of the school year.

Fortunately, children have a way of working out some difficulties almost by themselves. As Pat Vyas[29] tells it:

*The other children in the classroom have accepted Peter
beautifully. If there is any problem at all, it is that they
are a bit protective of him and tend to help him with
things he should be doing by himself. But they are very
supportive of him; when he shows off a new
accomplishment, they will greet it with shouts of joy and
run to the teacher to be sure she saw it, too.*

---

[29] Vyas, P. 1983. Just another little kid. In: T. Dougan, L. Isbell, and P. Vyas (eds.),
*We Have Been There: A Guidebook for Parents of People with Mental Retarda-
tion.* Abingdon Press, Nashville, TN.

If you have the opportunity to observe your child interacting in the preschool classroom, you may notice that your child is not interacting much with other children, or you may feel that he or she is being rejected by some of the more developmentally advanced children. Some parents find that, by detecting these subtle warning signals and by responding to their child's needs before any problems escalate, they can eliminate many of their own worries.

Learning To Coordinate and Monitor Services

Many parents find that it is difficult to adjust to working with a whole array of services and with the staff associated with their child's preschool. For example, they may notice inconsistencies in therapeutic or educational strategies recommended by the preschool teacher and by the child's therapist. Or, as is common with parents working outside of the home, there may be problems coordinating the child's preschool schedule with their own work schedule or with the activities of other family members. Be sure to bring up any questions or ideas you have on how to ensure that everyone involved—you, the teacher, and the program director—do not have schedule conflicts. Also, coordinating what you do at home (in terms of teaching or working with your child) with what the teacher does in class will help ensure that you are using consistent approaches. One mother describes how she increased the coordination between home and school:

Tim has emotional and behavioral problems that sometimes push me to my limit. Trying to get him to mind at home seemed to be a continuing battle. When I observed him at preschool, I realized that things seem to go better for him there. His teacher explained to me that they have clear classroom rules. Tim gets "timed out" [i.e., isolated from the rest of the class] if he breaks the rules. I realized that Tim was getting mixed messages, because the rules at school and at home were different. Tim's teacher helped me to make a rule chart at home that is the same as the one at school. She also taught me how to use time out. Now, Tim has the same

expectations and the same consequences for
misbehavior at school and at home. You wouldn't
believe how much his behavior has improved.

There are several strategies that you might use to coordinate and to monitor the various services delivered to your child at the preschool. Discuss with the teacher or program director how you might stay informed of your child's instructional program and the progress being made. When you have concerns, try to make it a practice to speak up and tell the teacher; don't wait until half the year is over to let the teacher know that you have questions about program quality or about your child's lack of progress. Some parents prefer to devise a specific method for ongoing communication, e.g., passing a notebook with comments about the day back and forth between home and school. A page in such a notebook is illustrated in Table 10.1. Other strategies for communicating with teachers are discussed in the final two chapters.

ARE YOU PREPARED?

You may not have the time, the inclination, or the need to follow the suggestions in this chapter. What *is* important is that you give some thought to these issues and concerns so that you can prepare yourself for a positive and satisfying preschool experience.

Table 10.1. Home-school notebook

October 2	October 30
Today Val succeeded in lacing up her own sneakers for the first time—looks like all those home teaching sessions paid off! Teacher	Please let me know when it is convenient for you to discuss some possible changes in Val's behavior program. I welcome your input! Teacher
Today we also worked on group skills, such as simple bowling and playing catch. Val followed all directions correctly, but she is still not able to throw and catch a small ball. We will continue with the large, lighter ball for a while. Teacher	
Val proudly showed us how she tied her shoes today! Parent	
Val's brothers are outside right now trying the ball-catching program. Parent	

HOW CAN YOU ENSURE THAT THE PRESCHOOL IS MEETING YOUR CHILD'S NEEDS AND YOUR OWN NEEDS?

Once you have selected a preschool and your child begins attending, you will have reached a milestone in making sure that your child has quality experiences during the early years. Many parents look forward to the transition period into a new program; they anticipate the establishment of a routine in which everything runs smoothly.

Such a routine usually does occur for parents and children; however, things do not always run smoothly. After your child enters the preschool program, issues may arise that you did not anticipate, or you may find that the program you expected to be implemented is not being carried out according to your expectations. On the other hand, you may find that the program meets your child's needs and your own needs much better than you would have predicted.

It is important for you to be prepared to monitor or to check on how the preschool program is helping your child. By staying in contact with what is happening at preschool, you can best ensure that your child's needs are met. Chapter 11 contains suggestions and ideas on how you can monitor the progress your child makes in the preschool.

Suppose, after you have tried out some of the monitoring techniques described in Chapter 11, you do actually find a problem. For example, suppose you discover that your child is not receiving the physical therapy program outlined in the IEP; or suppose that you find out that your child is socially isolated from the other children. What can you do about the situation? The purpose of Chapter 12 is to present strategies you might follow if you discover that either your child's needs or your needs are not being met. In the final chapter of the book, informal and formal techniques are suggested for resolving discrepancies or problems with your child's preschool program. Again, as with all suggestions in this book, you will need to adopt these techniques according to your own interaction style and preference.

Chapter 11

HOW CAN YOU MONITOR YOUR CHILD'S PROGRESS IN THE PRESCHOOL PROGRAM?

The focus of this chapter is the process of *monitoring,* which means to check your child's progress to identify both the benefits of the preschool experience and the areas of needed improvement. Many parents wonder why they should have to monitor their child's preschool program; after carefully exploring the available preschool programs and making a selection, they assume they can leave additional programming and decision making up to the preschool teacher. Sometimes things go very smoothly and the teacher is successful with the program. However, there are several very good reasons why you might want to check up on your child's program on a regular basis. For example, programming changes often do take place, and the teacher may be too busy or may have forgotten to inform you of them. Changes you should know about include: modifications in your child's behavior management program; alterations in the toilet-training schedule; an increased use of sign language by all of the children in the classroom; changes in the amount or type of special services your child is receiving; or changes in staffing. Also, if you are concerned about a lack of progress in your child's skill development, monitoring can sometimes provide explanations or reasons for it.

A more general reason for you to monitor your child's program is that many preschools simply do not systematically check on the progress of students, usually because of lack of teacher time or other available staff. If your child is in a publicly supported preschool in a state where preschool education is required by law, he or she should have an IEP. In this case, you should be able to count on an *annual* review of your child's progress in mastering goals and objectives; however, we would encourage you to meet with the teacher more often than annually—perhaps, every couple of months—to review how your child is doing. When you monitor your child's progress on the IEP, you can ask yourself the following questions:

1. Is the teacher following the programming and instructional strategies outlined in the IEP?

2. Is my child actually receiving the required specialized services?

3. Is this preschool classroom placement really appropriate for my child?

4. Is my child making the expected progress?

There are several reasons why the IEP (or your child's basic program of instruction if there is no formal IEP) may fall short of its intended goals. There may be a lack of funds for hiring specialized personnel, such as an occupational therapist. A parent whose daughter was starting public school kindergarten makes this statement:

One thing that still concerns me is that occupational therapy has been drastically overlooked in Sally's life. If she's ever going to learn how to take care of herself—get herself in and out of her wheelchair and things like that—she's going to have to have someone to work directly with her every day to teach her how. We specified that in her IEP, but I know the public schools do not have the staff to provide this. They have OTs [occupational therapists], but only on a consultant basis. So that's one thing I'll really have to follow up on. I think it's going to take parents' putting pressure on the school system to get this kind of service. Even the school will tell you that. Unless you express the need, they are not going to hire the extra staff and go the extra step to provide all that is necessary.

There are other reasons why your child's program of instruction may not be followed exactly. Your child's regular preschool teacher could become ill for a long period of time, which can be disruptive to the classroom routine. There could be a sudden increase in enrollment or a drop in staff, with the result being less individual teacher time for your child. There may also be other events using up available teacher time, such as the special needs of students in the class. All of these situations could be observed and understood by monitoring the preschool classroom on a regular basis.

STRATEGIES YOU CAN USE TO MONITOR YOUR CHILD'S PRESCHOOL PROGRAM

There are various strategies that are useful for gathering information about the actual programming and instruction that your child receives.

Classroom Observation

One of the most obvious and simple ways to gather information is to observe your child in the preschool setting. This can be done by sitting in the classroom, watching the children while they are playing outside, sitting in an observation room attached to the classroom (if one is available), or actually assisting the teacher as a helper in the classroom. You may already have done some informal classroom observation in preparing yourself for the preschool program. However, if you are planning to observe your child's classroom expressly for the purpose of monitoring the program, here are some considerations to keep in mind:

1. Give your child's teacher advance notice of your visit, and let him or her know how long you plan to stay.
2. While observing, keep all conversation with staff and children to a minimum; most teachers prefer a fairly inconspicuous observer.

3. Decide beforehand the specific activities you are going to observe (e.g., language instruction or playground activity) and why you are observing these. Some questions you should keep in mind as you observe are:

Can you observe any progress (in social, self-help, motor, cognitive, or language skills) in your child?

Do you see progress in the areas specifically noted in your child's IEP, in your discussions with the teacher, or in your assessment of your child's needs?

How does your child's progress in specific skill areas (such as language or gross motor skills) compare to the first day of preschool? To last month? To yesterday?

What positive behaviors or skills did you notice?

What negative behaviors were apparent?

What is your child's reaction to the program? Does the child seem to enjoy going?

4. If you think your child has a specific problem in class, you may want to arrange a visit to the classroom specifically to monitor the occurrence of the behavior or situation that concerns you. For instance, if you feel that your child may not be getting enough help, you could record the number of times in an hour that your child asks for help and receives it. Another strategy you might try would be to develop a simple checklist of needs from your child's IEP or from informal documentation. During observation you can check off those needs that are being met. For this type of record you might want to visit the classroom several times to get an accurate impression of the activities being provided by the preschool program. (The resources section contains some references that explain how to make such observations of your child, such as Anderson, Chitwood, and Hayden's *Negotiating the Special Education Maze* and *The Steps to Independence Series,* by Baker and his colleagues.)

5. Try to follow up your observations by having a conference with the teacher. You might use this opportunity to thank the teacher for allowing you to observe, to raise questions about what you observed, or to share your thoughts and feelings about your child's progress.

Anecdotal Records

You may want to record your observations and impressions so that you can analyze and interpret those impressions later. You can simply keep an anecdotal record of your general impressions—that is, take notes that describe activities in which your child engages, children with whom he or she plays, or how the teacher appears to interact with your child. Table 11.1 includes an example of an anecdotal record based on parent observations.

Notebook

In Chapter 10 the use of a notebook, passed back and forth between you and the teacher, was recommended to foster communication. You can also use this same notebook and feedback from the teacher as a means of monitoring some of your child's activities and progress.

Ask Your Child

Another means of gathering information about your child's preschool program is simply to discuss the program with your child (if he or she is able to communicate). Some issues that you could explore with your child are favorite activities, least favorite activities, friends played with, and the best part of each day. Your child's responses could alert you to strengths of the program and possible problems. For example, if your child tells you that favorite activities are those done alone (such as doing a puzzle, dressing, or looking at picture books) and he or she has no "best friends" or playmates, you may suspect a lack of social interaction with other children. If your child is physically handicapped and reports doing "nothing" on the playground, you might want to explore some adaptive physical education activities with the teacher. Talking with other parents of children at the preschool to determine their children's reactions to the school program can also yield useful information.

Ask Your Child's Teacher

A major source of information about your child's progress in the preschool program is, of course, your child's teacher. The

Table 11.1. Anecdotal record

What I observed	Later interpretations or impressions of what I observed
10/18/82; 10 a.m. Val playing with Donald, a hearing-impaired preschooler who has more advanced motor skills than Val, and with Cindy, a nonhandicapped child.	I'm delighted that the mainstreaming concept is working! Cindy is actually helping Val, and both girls are making an effort to communicate with Donald.
11/5/82; 2 p.m. Val having a mild temper tantrum, because she cannot operate the toys she selected to play with.	Val still has that high level of frustration! I need to talk to her teacher a bit more about strategies for managing her occasional outbursts.

teacher serves as the central person in communicating with you, your child, administrators, other parents and children, and any specialized support personnel. It is helpful if the teacher perceives you as a concerned parent who also understands the needs of teachers. As a result of your monitoring, let the teacher know the things you particularly like. Teachers, too, appreciate praise and reinforcement. A preschool teacher emphasizes this point as follows:

I always look forward to getting a note from Denise's parents. When they see progress in any of her skills, they have a real knack for making me feel good about it. My last note said, "Denise won the 'neatest eater' award at dinner last night. It never would have happened without all the help you have given her. We are very grateful that the neatest eater has the neatest teacher. Thanks for your help and concern."

The next section includes many suggestions for teacher communication.

COMMUNICATING WITH TEACHERS ABOUT YOUR CHILD'S PROGRESS

You should try to plan opportunities for ongoing communication with teachers to discuss your child's progress. You will want to ask teachers how they document your child's progress. They may use formal tests or observations to determine how well your child completes tasks in the classroom. They may then record these results in a variety of ways, including checklists, charts, or graphs. Remember that specifying evaluation procedures is a required component of the IEP, if your child has one. You should request that teachers share the results of all evaluations with you.

Although we have emphasized the benefits of maintaining open channels of communication between parents and professionals in general, it is important to learn how open communication can be an effective monitoring technique. To make communications between you and the teacher successful, you need to be open to other viewpoints, to give positive feedback to teachers, to state your own perspectives, and perhaps to take notes on major points so that you can clarify any questions later. It is also important for you to be assertive in stating your own perspective, in a clear and direct manner without being overbearing. One teacher described a parent as follows: "She's easy to work with and she knows her rights." When told by a friend about this comment, the parent felt highly complimented, because she had worked many years to get to that point where she could stand up for what she knew to be right, without going overboard. For her, the key was "staying calm, sticking to your guns, and knowing the law." This parent had obviously impressed, but not offended, the preschool teachers with her knowledge about the law, parental rights, and program issues.

Such communication can take place during informal interactions, such as drop-off and pick-up times at your child's preschool. This can be an excellent source of monitoring your child's activities; however, time is often short and many interruptions occur. In addition, parents who work outside the home may not have this opportunity if a friend or babysitter transports the child to preschool.

Formal opportunities for communicating about child progress can include meetings at school, home visits, or telephone conversations. To review your child's progress in an in-depth manner, it is a good idea to schedule some formal contacts throughout the year. The number of formal contacts you choose to make with your child's teacher depends upon many factors: whether you feel confident or doubtful that your child's needs are being met; your own time limits and the teacher's time availability; and your own preference and the teacher's preferences for communication.

When planning meetings to discuss your child's progress, it is important to carefully consider your preferences. Do you like home visits or not? In light of your daily schedule, when is it most convenient for you to schedule conferences? Do you feel confident going to conferences alone, or do you prefer to have your spouse or a friend go along? After you have considered your own preferences, it is just as important to consider those of the teacher. One preschool teacher comments:

Parents forget how busy teachers are. When I ask parents to come in for a conference, they sometimes tell me they

*can't come during the day because they work. I am
tempted to say back to them, "I know how it is; I work,
too." One parent told me she wanted to meet at night.
That might be convenient for her, but it is not
convenient for me. Evenings are for my family; I don't
think I should have to leave my own children at night to
have parent conferences.*

The more people who are required or who desire to attend
such a meeting, the harder it is to settle on a time convenient
for everyone. When scheduling meetings during regular preschool hours becomes a major problem, you might want to try
one of the following alternatives.

Conference Phone Call

When more than two individuals need to get together to discuss
issues related to your child, a "phone call get-together" can
sometimes be arranged. With operator assistance, you can have
several parties (for example, you, your spouse, your child's
teacher, and your child's physical therapist) on the telephone at
once.

Arranging Casual Meeting Places

One mother of a handicapped preschooler told us she went
jogging two mornings a week with her child's teacher. It was
during those times that stories and reports of child progress
could be shared. This mother found it very easy and comfortable to share her worries or concerns in this informal style.
Inviting your child's teacher to meet with you on the tennis
court, at the health club, or over a cup of coffee (all during
nonschool hours, of course) can be equally productive.

Meeting on Weekends

If all else fails, and you cannot attend meetings during the week,
there are still two days left to consider. A cup of coffee together
on a Saturday morning or a quick visit to your child's preschool
Saturday afternoon might be alternatives. Of course, your convenience as well as that of the teacher must be considered.

Conferences with Persons Other Than the Teacher

Specific meetings or conferences with individuals other than your child's teacher can also help you to monitor your child's progress in the preschool program. You may find it helpful to set up conferences with the preschool director or administrator, with some of the classroom aides, or with your child's speech and physical therapists. Sometimes these people have more flexibility than teachers in their daily schedules; thus, it may be easier to schedule a meeting with them. If you are checking up on a specific problem, such as the frequency of temper tantrums, or progress in a specific skill area like the use of phrases and sentences, you might also confer, informally, with your child's babysitter or with other family members.

Meeting in Groups

Finally, if you are so inclined, you can use the collective effort of a group to monitor your child's progress. By becoming active in advocacy groups, by participating on preschool advisory boards, and by attending PTA-type activities, you may be able to gain additional information about your child's program and progress.

DEALING WITH CONCERNS IDENTIFIED THROUGH MONITORING

After you have monitored your child's program or progress, you may have concerns that need to be addressed. For example, you may feel that your child is not making adequate progress in language development (vocabulary doesn't seem to be increasing) or in social skills development (the child still does not interact with other children and make friends). Concerns may also originate from the quantity and quality of related services or the overall appropriateness of the program for your child. How can you actually use the information you have collected to make changes in your child's preschool program? The next chapter includes an array of strategies for you to consider in making requests for changes.

Chapter 12

WHAT DO YOU DO WHEN YOUR CHILD'S NEEDS AND YOUR NEEDS ARE NOT BEING MET?

In considering the problem of unmet needs, perhaps the best advice is to prevent problems before they occur. Numerous strategies, which have been described in this book, are helpful in preventing such problems. You should invest energy and time in initially locating a preschool that has a high probability of success in meeting your child's needs. Through careful communication, you can ensure that the teachers are aware of your child's needs and your own needs. By becoming an active participant in the program-planning process, you can ensure that the result is appropriate to your child's needs. In addition, maintaining ongoing communication with your child's teachers and with other preschool staff members helps to keep staff members up-to-date about your concerns. It is helpful for you consistently to use positive communication in letting the teacher and preschool staff know which of their efforts are particularly helpful to your child and to you. At times during your child's preschool experience, however, you may feel that your child's needs or your needs are not being met. Consider the following situations that two families found themselves in:

Kathy Allen resided in a state where preschool for handicapped children was mandated. However, she was frustrated because her son's publicly supported preschool did not provide transportation. Her four-year-old son, Kevin, used a wheelchair, which was very heavy. His mother knew that the school system had a bus equipped with a lift. Kathy Allen finally went to the Director of Special Education and complained about the school's failure to provide transportation for her son. She declared that she would initiate a due process hearing if necessary. Within a week Kevin was being transported to and from preschool.

Mr. and Mrs. Wood were concerned about their daughter's lack of language skills. Her private preschool agreed to provide her with half an hour per week of speech training or therapy. However, their daughter did not seem to be making any progress at all and the Woods felt she needed more hours of therapy. Both parents work full-time and neither one is able to take their daughter, Grace, to a private speech therapist two or three times a week. They knew that the preschool did not legally owe them any more speech therapy, yet they wondered how some additional hours might be negotiated. They were amazed and delighted when a carefully planned meeting with the preschool therapist resulted in an additional two hours per week of therapy for Grace [i.e., half an hour per day].

In the first case above, the need of Kevin's mother to have Kevin transported was clearly not being met. However, Kathy Allen knew her legal rights and was able to make a firm, reasonable demand of the school system. The Woods found that neither their needs nor their child's needs were being met, yet they had no legal basis to back up their request for services. Instead, they tried a number of alternative strategies and came to a satisfactory solution. This chapter contains a review of the types of strategies available to you when you find that your needs or your child's needs are not being met.

REVIEW YOUR OWN EXPECTATIONS AND NEEDS

It is important to realize that most parents do not find a program that can meet every child need and every parent need. That is one of the reasons for you to think about your child's needs and your needs, as suggested in Chapters 2 and 3. The process of selecting a preschool program for your child requires that you prioritize those needs. In other words, you will have decided which needs are most important for the preschool to meet (non-negotiable ones), which are of moderate importance, and which are of least importance.

When you identify needs that are not being met by your child's program, you need to consider where those needs fall in your priorities. You may find that certain needs are least important (for instance, the need for your child to learn "k" sounds) and can be met in other ways. If so, you may decide to invest your time and energy in having the need met outside of the preschool, for example, by a speech therapist. On the other hand, if the need is very important or moderately important (i.e., the need for your child to be toilet trained), you most likely will decide that the need should be systematically addressed when you speak with the teacher and with the preschool staff.

PLANNING FOR A MEETING WITH PRESCHOOL STAFF

There are several approaches you may want to consider taking if your needs or your child's needs are not being met. The first is simply to talk to the teacher alone, or to a whole range of people, in a private meeting or in a conference format. It is important to remember that most problems or difficulties can be resolved at this level and do not require more intensive actions. Later in this chapter other strategies are outlined (IEP adjustments, informal negotiations, due process hearing, and political advocacy) that may be available to you.

Many parents find it difficult and anxiety provoking to talk with their child's teacher or with other staffmembers about unmet needs or concerns. You should plan in advance before you meet with preschool staffmembers to talk about a problem. An important part of this planning is to identify your needs and your child's needs in a precise way. It is impossible to discuss needs or concerns effectively if your own perspective is vague and unfocused. To avoid this, write down the unmet needs or issues that are concerning you. As examples:

You are concerned that your child is learning about dinosaurs instead of about self-help skills.

You want your child to learn to communicate, nonvocally if necessary, and you feel that he or she is not benefiting from the teacher's emphasis on phonics.

You cannot come to most parent meetings and group teacher conferences because they are scheduled during your work hours. You have a strong need, however, to discuss your concerns with other parents.

You need advice from the teacher or feedback from other parents about problems between your handicapped child and his or her siblings.

After you have listed such needs and concerns, identify and write down at least two and possibly more ways in which you think that the preschool could successfully meet each need. As you list solutions to each unmet need, identify your most preferred solution, then your second and third choices. Remember to propose workable and functional solutions, considering the teacher time and resources available for your child. If your requests are unreasonable, they will probably be rejected by the preschool staff members. Table 12.1 provides a review of this process.

You may also want to prepare an outline or write out what you plan to say during the meeting. After you write down your thoughts and organize them in a logical order, you may want to role play what you are going to say with a friend, or tape it and listen to yourself. It's important for you to do whatever you need to do to help you feel secure and confident when you talk with your child's teacher or with other staffmembers.

It is important to resolve your problem at the level as close to its origin as possible. You should consider the hierarchy for decision making in your child's preschool. In public schools, this is likely to be the teacher, principal, director of special

Table 12.1. Planning for a teacher conference

Unmet needs	Strategies to try	Talking to the teacher
I. No transportation for your child, who is in a wheelchair.	A) Write a letter to the Director of Special Education to request transportation on an accessible bus.	Enlist the support of your child's teacher; ask him or her to also contact the Director of Special Education.
	B) Continue driving the child yourself, but get daily help lifting your child into and out of your car.	Ask the teacher if one of the classroom aides could be regularly available to assist you.
II. Inadequate provision of speech therapy services for your child.	A) Request an IEP meeting to increase the amount of speech therapy your child receives.	State your reasons; explain exactly why you think more speech therapy is needed.
	B) Take your child to a private speech therapist after school.	If you do pay for outside speech services, coordinate your home program with your child's school program; let the teacher know how therapy is going.

education, assistant superintendent, or superintendent. In a private preschool, the chain of command may only be the teacher and the program director. Move up the hierarchy in talking with persons only when previous attempts for resolution have not helped you.

Other parents whose children have been in the preschool are an excellent source of ideas, advice, and suggestions for solving problems. Parent organizations like the ARC (Association for Retarded Citizens) may have a list of persons who frequently help parents resolve educational problems, and such organizations might be useful to you. If you have had an independent evaluation of your child by a certified professional not employed by the school system, you may want to ask this professional for advice on the needs or concerns you have identified. Asking the evaluator to attend the meeting with you is also an alternative. If you have any medical or school records for your child related to your concerns, be sure to gather these in preparation for the meeting.

SCHEDULING A MEETING

After documenting your concerns and identifying the appropriate persons with whom to meet, you need to schedule a meeting time. You should schedule a meeting time far enough in advance to ensure that it is convenient for everyone. When you schedule meetings, let other people involved know about the nature of your concerns. You may want to send them a letter in advance that states the purpose of the meeting and the issues you would like to address. This approach will ensure that they have adequate planning time to consider various alternatives for problem resolution.

CONDUCTING THE MEETING

There are several points to remember when you actually meet with school personnel. First, introductions of all people present should take place. Although this may sound trivial, sometimes meetings are conducted without participants having been introduced. In terms of communication style, it is important that you state your concerns clearly and concisely. It may help to bring the list of unmet needs you have prepared (as suggested earlier in this chapter). Listen very carefully to the viewpoints of the preschool staff, but by all means feel free to ask questions. As you talk, identify and discuss points of agreement and disagreement. Be sure to discuss the various alternative solutions to your child's unmet needs, and be prepared to propose a solution satisfactory to you, based on the alternatives you have identified. Discuss areas in which you are willing to compromise and those in which you cannot make compromises. In this manner you may be able to reach a solution satisfactory to all parties. Finally, use time at the meeting efficiently, and if you are short on time, let others know.

If your child's preschool is required by law to produce an IEP and one has been prepared for your child, you can schedule the type of meeting described above expressly for the purpose of reviewing or revising the IEP. You might wish to refer back to Chapter 7 for suggestions for participating in the IEP meeting.

STILL NO SOLUTION?
THE DUE PROCESS HEARING

It may happen that a satisfactory solution has not been reached through informal negotiations between you and the preschool staff. If your child is in a privately supported preschool, you have no *guarantee* of an appropriate education. Your best alternative may be to withdraw your child from the program and to find another one where the child's needs are more likely to be met.

If no satisfactory solutions can be agreed upon through informal negotiations and your child is in a public school program, you have the option of initiating a due process hearing. Unlike informal negotiation, in which two parties try to work out their own disagreements, in a due process hearing the decision-making authority is put in the hands of an outside, presumably impartial, individual. The actual due process hearing is typically a more formal procedure than a negotiation conference. As discussed in Chapter 6, Public Law 94–142 guarantees the right of participants in due process hearings to:

   1. Be accompanied and advised by counsel and by individuals with special knowledge or training with respect to the problems of handicapped children.

2. Present evidence, confront, cross-examine, and compel the attendance of witnesses.

3. Prohibit the introduction of any evidence at the hearing that has not been disclosed to the other party at least five days before the hearing.

4. Obtain a written or electronic verbatim record of the hearing.

5. Obtain written findings of facts and decision.[30]

When may a due process hearing be initiated? A due process hearing may be initiated if you believe the school system has violated any of your rights or your child's rights. According to a National Association of State Directors of Special Education report,[31] 40% of due process hearings in one state dealt with placement; in every instance reported, parents were requesting a private placement. In 60% of the cases, the hearing issue related to the appropriateness of the child's current program.

Who is present at a due process hearing? The usual participants include the parents, sometimes their child, their lawyer or advocate if they have one, and any witnesses testifying on their behalf. Similarly, the school system staff are present, in addition to their legal counsel and any necessary witnesses. A hearing officer must be present, because he or she determines the outcome of the case, based on the evidence and testimony presented by both parties. The school system is responsible for appointing a hearing officer who is not an employee of the system and who is impartial.

What happens during a hearing? The actual procedure varies from one school system to another. (The details of a hearing are clearly explained in Anderson, Chitwood, and Hayden's book, *Negotiating the Special Education Maze,* which is cited in the resource section.) Basically, the hearing officer opens the hearing, then both sides present evidence, witnesses, and clos-

---

[30] *Federal Register.* 1977. August 23, 1977, p. 42495. U.S. Government Printing Office, Washington, DC.

[31] National Association of State Directors of Special Education. 1978. *The Implementation of Due Process in Massachusetts.* National Association of State Directors of Special Education, Washington, DC.

ing statements. The hearing officer then is allowed a 45-day period to make a decision and to mail a written copy of the decision to both parties. If you are dissatisfied with the decision, you can appeal for a review of the hearing at the state level.

How can a due process hearing affect the parent-school relationship? Generally, parents who become involved in hearings have already had numerous contacts with their child's school, either through informal meetings or through IEP conferences. The quality of such parent-school contacts during hearings can be affected by the person at the school responsible for interacting with parents, the way in which parents are contacted, the organization of the hearing itself, and the actual formality of the hearing. There are costs and benefits to be weighed before initiating the due process hearing. Hearings can be expensive in terms of time and money. Frequently, parents obtain the services of a lawyer, which greatly adds to the cost of a hearing. What is perhaps most disconcerting is research, such as that from one state, indicating that the issue that led to the hearing was still not adequately resolved even after the hearing. Many parents who have been through due process report negative reactions:[32]

> It's very expensive in terms of time and money and highly unlikely to achieve the desired results.
>
> The hearing gets you so upset, confused, and disturbed that you don't know what you think.
>
> It was a total waste of time and money. It was very draining emotionally. I was physically sick the next day.

On the other hand, due process hearings have proved to be a positive experience for many parents. It can allow for correction of improper decisions or procedures related to the appropriateness of the handicapped child's education. One parent comments: "The procedure is very adequate. It worked, although it was expensive in legal fees." Other parents have emphasized the value of due process as a strategy for keeping

---

[32] Strickland, B. 1982. Perceptions of parents and school representatives regarding their relationship before, during, and after the due process hearing. Doctoral dissertation, University of North Carolina, Chapel Hill.

school officials on their toes. As expressed by a parent who had initiated a hearing: "If the school knows parents will stand up for themselves, parents will be treated with more respect and will stand a better chance of getting what they need."

A final benefit of following through on due process procedures when the appropriateness of your child's education is in question is that it gives you the assurance that you have done everything you can to improve the situation. This perspective was provided by a parent who said: "I can look at my child now and at least say I tried to do what was right."

It is obvious that many factors must be considered in the determination of whether a due process hearing will be a viable alternative for ensuring that your child's needs are met. Local parent organizations are often useful if you are considering a due process hearing. Such organizations may be able to help you prepare for a hearing or advise you concerning the likelihood of success of the hearing. They may also know of local and state resources for legal aid and are often effective in legal and political advocacy efforts. Many parents have found that their efforts are most effective if they work in groups. Gerta Harvey[33] expresses this feeling when describing her involvement in a local Association for Retarded Citizens unit:

The role of the parent becomes one of organizer, one of watchdog, one of prodder. Do our school administrators, our state legislators, our city and county officials, our church leaders have the best interests of our children in mind? If not, as parents we ask ourselves, "What can we do?" We find that one of the strongest powers on earth is "parent power." To be effective this power has to be used by a united group.

Working as a group can provide emotional and physical support and can increase one's political clout; it may also mean that, at a later point in time, it may be possible for an individual

---

[33] Harvey, G. 1983. They want to help but they don't know how. In: T. Dougan, L. Isbell, and P. Vyas (eds.), *We Have Been There: A Guidebook for Parents of People with Mental Retardation*. Abingdon Press, Nashville, TN.

within that group to take a break without feeling like the cause is being abandoned. The parents of a blind preschooler, who were intensively involved both in advocacy work and in the organization of a parent's political group, gave this type of interchange of energy as one of the reasons for their current commitment:

We're new at this and still have a lot of energy. We know we'll reach a point of burnout; but if there's an ongoing group recruiting fresh energy, where we can get support—a group watchdogging the system when we may be unable to—then the energy we're expending now will be a worthwhile investment.

We are moving in a direction in which the needs and feelings of handicapped individuals are being more openly discussed in our society. Let us hope that one day parent advocates can make assumptions of quality about the services in which handicapped children are enrolled. As parents of young handicapped children, sometimes it may be impossible for you to recognize the vast improvement in educational services and the increase in educational options that has occurred over the last 20 years. Much of this improvement can be credited to the parents of handicapped sons and daughters who are now adults. These parents advocated long and hard for the benefits enjoyed by the next generation of families and their handicapped children. Although we have come a long way, there are still improvements to be made to ensure quality of life for our children. Individually and collectively we have both a challenge and an opportunity to participate in the process.

RESOURCES

CRITERIA FOR INCLUSION

Listed below are recommended readings, three to five per topic, which you may want to review. Many of these selections are cited in the text of this book. The following criteria were used for selecting an item: 1) the material should be written in a clear, readable style; 2) it should be of particular interest to parents of handicapped children; 3) it should be readily available (wherever possible specific ordering information is included, otherwise the item can be obtained at a library or directly from the publisher); and 4) the item has been read or used by other parents and professionals and has received a positive review. Also included under appropriate categories are lists of organizations that you might be interested in contacting or joining.

EARLY INTERVENTION

Much has been written about the beneficial effects of early intervention efforts for handicapped and high-risk infants. If you are interested in reading about some of the research and rationale for early intervention, the references included here are appropriate. Also included are a few references to books on toys and play, to emphasize that simple play with your child is a type of informal intervention that you, as well as the teacher, can provide.

Caldwell, B., and Stedman, D.J. 1977. *Infant Education: A Guide for Helping Handicapped Children in the First Three Years.* Walker Company, New York.
This book contains a review of the work done on early

intervention throughout the United States, primarily during the 1970s. Specific projects are described, and particular attention is devoted to the role of parent involvement in each program. The book is paperback and fairly easy, non-technical reading.

Cook, R.E., and Armbruster, V.B. 1983. *Adapting Early Child-hood Curricula: Suggestions for Meeting Special Needs.* C.V. Mosby Company, St. Louis, MO.
This extremely comprehensive book is intended to provide teachers, parents, and paraprofessionals with a wealth of information and techniques for adapting a regular early childhood education curriculum to any preschool child with special needs. Some of the useful topics included are a thorough overview of various curricular approaches (e.g., Montessori, Behavioral, Piagetian, and Developmental) and specific descriptions of assessment, instructional strategies, and parent programs. Of particular relevance is the chapter on working with parents, which contains a variety of innovative approaches and suggestions, such as how to foster productive relationships with parents who do not speak English or who are themselves handicapped.

Connor, F.P. 1981. Perspective on early childhood programs. *The Exceptional Parent,* 1(1), 53–56.
This short article provides a brief rationale for early intervention. The author describes types of parent involvement, specific programs, and potential problems in continuing early intervention programs in some states.

Tjossem, T.D. (ed.). 1976. *Intervention Strategies with High Risk Infants and Young Children.* University Park Press, Baltimore.
This book contains a collection of research papers on many aspects of early intervention. Descriptions of a variety of programs serving children with different handicaps are included. Related issues also addressed include costs, parent involvement, and policy. It is a more academic version than the above references and is extremely comprehensive. Par-

ents interested in reviewing data on the developmental
progress of children in early intervention programs can find
that type of information in this book.

White, B.L. 1975. *The First Three Years of Life.* Prentice-Hall,
Inc., Englewood Cliffs, NJ.
This book contains one of the most vivid, accurate, and
interesting accounts of normal or near-normal development
during the first three years of a child's life. Although issues
pertaining to handicapped children are not addressed, many
parents still find it useful, because it provides details of
development as well as discussion of topics related to child
rearing (such as sibling rivalry, assessment, and obtaining
professional services for children).

TOYS AND PLAY

Baker, B.L., Brightman, A.J., and Blacher, J. 1983. *Steps to Independence Series: Play Skills.* Research Press, Champaign, IL.
This is the ninth in the series of parent training manuals by
Baker and his colleagues. This particular manual is written
exclusively for use by parents in working with their handicapped child at home. The manual includes instructions for
parents on how to assess their child's level of play skill, how
to teach specific skills, and how to increase the difficulty of
the skills taught. The curriculum includes "get ready" play
skills, independent types of play, play with others, and group
games. Activities are covered for young children with different handicaps, including those with severe delays.

Newson, J., and Newson, E. 1979. *Toys and Playthings in Development and Remediation.* 1st Ed. Pantheon Books, New York.
This book is a comprehensive guide to selecting playthings
suited to any young child's particular needs (handicapped or
nonhandicapped children). The text illustrates how toys may
become tools for assessment and remediation as well as for
play. The focus of the book is on the child's developmental
level rather than age per se, which makes it especially appropriate as a guide for you and for your handicapped
preschooler.

PARENT TRAINING

The following is a selection of training manuals and books that have been used by parents interested in teaching their handicapped child at home. Some of these references are for complete, self-instructional programs in certain skill areas; others describe the general process of teaching.

Baker, B.L., Brightman, A.J., Carroll, N.B., Heifetz, B.B., and Hinshaw, S.P. 1978. *Steps to Independence: A Skills Training Series for Children with Special Needs. Speech and Language: Level 1 and Speech and Language: Level 2.* Research Press, Champaign, IL.
Baker, B.L., Brightman, A.J., Heifetz, L.J., and Murphy, D. *Steps to Independence Series: Behavior Problems,* 1976; *Early Self-help Skills,* 1976; *Intermediate Self-help Skills,* 1976; *Advanced Self-help Skills,* 1976; *Toilet Training,* 1977; *Trainer's Guide,* 1976. Research Press, Champaign, IL.
Baker, B.L., Brightman, A.J., and Hinshaw, S.P. 1980. *Steps to Independence Series: Toward Independent Living.* Research Press, Champaign, IL.
These manuals were written specifically for parents of handicapped children who are interested in teaching skills to their child at home. Each one incorporates a behavior modification approach and has been validated through use with hundreds of families during years of research. The manuals are easy to read and dotted throughout with humorous, relevant drawings that help make the entire teaching program seem like fun. Each manual is independent of the others and teaches a different aspect of development. Although the focus is on teaching children with mental retardation, the manuals have been used with groups of parents of blind children, of severely handicapped children, and of children with spina bifida. In these cases, group leaders may work together with parents to adapt the materials and teaching instructions (e.g., using large-print materials for visually impaired children or combining signing, showing, and guiding for hearing-impaired or severely handicapped children).

Jeffree, D.M., McConkey, R., and Hewson, S. 1982. *Teaching the Handicapped Child: A Guide for Parents and Teachers.* Prentice-Hall, Inc., Englewood Cliffs, NJ.
This book is somewhat more general than the manuals by Baker et al., but does offer parents as well as professionals a systematic approach to teaching a handicapped child. Rather than giving information on teaching specific skills, the book provides information on choosing teaching objectives, making assessments, selecting the most effective teaching technique, and evaluating child progress.

Luce, S.C., and Christian, W.P. 1981. *How to Reduce Autistic and Severely Maladaptive Behaviors.* H & H Enterprises, Inc., Lawrence, KS.
This short book is intended for parents and teachers of children with autism and severe behavior problems. The manual provides reviews of behavior management procedures for reducing maladaptive behaviors, such as extinction, time out, and contingent reinforcement loss. An explanation of how to use these procedures is included, along with a description of specific behaviors one might want to reduce.

Maloney, P.L. 1981. *Practical Guidance for Parents of the Visually Handicapped Preschooler.* Charles C Thomas, Publisher, Springfield, IL.
In fewer than 100 pages, the author of this book provides a wealth of information to make living with a visually handicapped preschooler easier. Although this is not a training manual per se, it does contain practical suggestions for teaching your child using ordinary household objects, for involving other family members, and for locating sources of special help for visually handicapped children.

Patterson, G.R. 1976. *Living with Children. New Methods for Parents and Teachers.* Research Press, Champaign, IL.
This book is aimed toward assisting parents of both normal and problem children to deal with situations that may arise in any family. The book requires a minimum of reading,

because it is written in the form of programmed instruction. Topics taught to the reader are: 1) how children learn; 2) how to change undesirable behavior; 3) normal child problems; and 4) specific problems (such as the child who steals or who is coercive).

Pearlman, L., and Scott, K.A. 1981. *Raising the Handicapped Child.* Prentice-Hall, Inc., Englewood Cliffs, NJ.
This book is included in order to provide a different perspective on parent training—one that is not so behavioral. Some typical behavior problems are reviewed in the book, but the focus is on more emotional or affective issues involved in living with a child who has behavioral or learning problems. Some interesting topics included are: 1) alternative living arrangements for a handicapped child; 2) financial considerations; and 3) facts versus myths about special children.

PARENTAL SUPPORT

A number of books have been written by or about parents and families of handicapped children. The following publications have been selected because they represent personal accounts as well as informational resources for parents.

Dougan, T., Isbell, L., and Vyas, P. 1983. *We Have Been There: A Guidebook for Parents of People with Mental Retardation.* Abingdon Press, Nashville, TN.
This publication is a "guidebook for parents of people with mental retardation." Each article or chapter is written by either a parent of a mentally retarded child, or by an individual who shares a particularly unique relationship with a retarded child. For example, in one section a parent and a teacher write a chapter about the same child; in another, a brother and a sister write about living with a handicapped sibling. The book is candid, educational, and enlightening. Each chapter is composed of rather short accounts or articles covering a range of topics, such as living with a preschooler, brothers and sisters, the future, perspectives on

getting appropriate services, and emotional experiences, such as anger or looking back.

Featherstone, H. 1981. *A Difference in the Family: Living with a Disabled Child.* Penguin Books, New York.
Unlike the previous reference, this book is not a collection of essays, but one author's account of experiences living with a handicapped or disabled child. Featherstone writes as the parent of a severely handicapped child, and, as such, has much insight into the difficulties faced by parents. Chapters include topics like anger or guilt and contain both Featherstone's reflections and quotations from other parents. Excellent discussions of the impact of the handicapped child on the entire family and adaptation to the special needs of the child are included. These discussions combine a solid theoretical approach to concepts with insightful embellishment through the personal experience of the author.

Harrison, H., and Kositsky, A. 1983. *The Premature Baby Book.* St. Martin's Press, New York.
Written by the parent of a premature baby, who is now a handicapped young boy, this may well become *the* book on premature babies. It is full of up-to-date facts, figures, and research on prematurity. The book is extremely readable, partly because case studies and accounts written by parents of premature infants are used to illustrate many technical points. After reading this book, one feels very knowledgeable about the care and development of premature infants.

Murphy, A.T. 1981. *Special Children, Special Parents: Personal Issues with Handicapped Children.* Prentice-Hall, Inc., Englewood Cliffs, NJ.
This book consists largely of quotes from parents. Each chapter focuses on a particular emotion or action, taking parents through the gamut of feelings and thoughts they may have about raising a handicapped child. Reassuring maxims, quotations, and passages from a diversity of sources, including philosophy, poetry, history, and art, offer the parent support in trying to overcome frustration, anger, guilt, doubts, and anxieties.

Turnbull, A.P., and Turnbull, H.R. 1978. *Parents Speak Out: Views from the Other Side of the Two-way Mirror.* Charles E. Merrill Publishing Co., Columbus, OH.
Parents Speak Out is an edited text containing contributions by parents of handicapped children who are all also professionals in the mental retardation/mental health fields. Each chapter is a first-hand account of what it is like discovering that one has a handicapped child, interacting with the service delivery system, and living with day-to-day problems as well as dealing with future considerations. As a whole, the book is warm yet firm, optimistic yet realistic, poignant yet factual, and serious yet humorous. In addition to being favorably reviewed by parents, it is also frequently used in college courses to sensitize students in education and other helping professions to the special needs of parents with handicapped children.

Perske, R., and Perske, M. 1981. *Hope for the Families: New Directions for Parents of Persons with Retardation or Other Developmental Disabilities.* Abingdon Press, Nashville, TN.
This book is intended for parents of children with special problems, but every parent or professional can benefit from reading it. It contains chapters with information on various topics, such as normalization, advocacy, parental expectations, parental response to initial diagnosis, and issues pertaining to sexual development. However, the book is more than just a compendium of information—the authors offer advice to parents and raise difficult questions sensitively. Illustrations by Martha Perske enliven the text.

MAINSTREAMING

Today there are probably more books available on mainstreaming than on any other topic in special education. The references below were selected in order to provide you with information on mainstreaming preschoolers with specific types of handicaps, as well as information on mainstreaming at the school-age level.

Allen, K.E. 1980. *Mainstreaming in Early Childhood Education.* Delmar Publishers, Albany, NY.
This book contains very straightforward, clearly written descriptions of the typical preschool mainstreaming classroom. Such information can be very helpful for parents in orienting them prior to their child's actual enrollment in a mainstreamed classroom.

Hart, V. 1980. *Mainstreaming Children with Special Needs.* Longman, Inc., New York.
This text is similar to the book cited above, but differs in one important respect—it deals with issues in mainstreaming in general, not just at the preschool or early childhood level. Parents interested in a longer range perspective on mainstreaming should find this book helpful.

Mainstreaming Preschoolers. Superintendent of Documents, U.S. Government Printing Office, Washington, DC.
Each of these eight manuals provides details about procedures and techniques for mainstreaming handicapped preschoolers into Head Start classrooms. Each manual covers a different handicap and is written by a different set of authors.

Alonso, L., Moor, P.M., Raynor, S., Von Hippel, C.S., and Baer, S. *Mainstreaming Preschoolers: Children with Visual Handicaps* (GPO #017–092—3030—8).

Hayden, A.H., Smith, R.K., Von Hippel, C.S., and Baer, S.A. *Mainstreaming Preschoolers: Children with Learning Disabilities* (GPO #017–092–3035–9).

Healy, A., McAreavey, P., Von Hippel, C.S., and Jones, S.H. *Mainstreaming Preschoolers: Children with Health Impairments* (GPO #017–092–3031–6).

Kiernan, S.S., Connor, F.P., Von Hippel, C.S., and Jones, S.H. *Mainstreaming Preschoolers: Children with Orthopedic Handicaps* (GPO #017–092–3034–1).

LaPorta, R.A., McGee, D.I., Simmons-Martin, A., Vorce, E., Von Hippel, C.S., and Donovan, J. *Mainstreaming Preschoolers with Hearing Impairments* (GPO #017–092–3032–4).

Lasher, M.G., Mattick, I., Perkins, F.J., Von Hippel, C.S., and Hailey, L.G. *Mainstreaming Preschoolers: Children with Emotional Disturbances* (GPO #017–092–3036–7).

Liebergott, J., Favors, A., Von Hippel, C.S., and Needleman, H. *Mainstreaming Preschoolers: Children with Speech and Language Impairments* (GPO #017–092–3033–2).

Lynch, E.W., Simms, B.H., Von Hippel, C.S., and Shuchat, J. *Mainstreaming Preschoolers: Children with Mental Retardation* (GPO #017–092–3029–4).

Koegel, R. 1981. *How to Integrate Autistic and Other Severely Handicapped Children into a Classroom.* H & H Enterprises, Lawrence, KS.
This short book is part of a series relating to more severely handicapped children. Parents of autistic children may find the explanations of behavioral programming and classroom instruction reassuring. The book contains some technical details in a readable format.

Perske, R. 1980. *New Life in the Neighborhood: How Persons with Retardation and Other Disabilities Can Help Make a Good Community Better.* Abingdon Press, Nashville, TN.
Perske's books always have a very human touch; in this one he deals factually with normalization and mainstreaming in the community at large. This book, too, is illustrated with drawings. Parents interested in future placements of their own children in the community should find this text enlightening.

New Friends. Manual and Notebook. 1983. Chapel Hill Training Outreach Program, Chapel Hill, NC.
This is a preschool-kindergarten level curriculum designed to help educators provide accurate information about various disabilities to young children and families of children with special needs. The program provides instructions for teaching parents and teachers to make dolls with various disabilities and instructions on how to use them with children.

ADVOCACY AND LEGAL ISSUES

Although many legal issues, especially as they pertain to pre-school-aged children, are discussed in this book, the following references have been included for those parents who wish to read further. This section also includes a list of advocacy organizations and addresses, which should be particularly helpful for parents wishing to form an advocacy group.

Anderson, W., Chitwood, S., and Hayden, D. 1982. *Negotiating the Special Education Maze.* Prentice-Hall, Inc., Englewood Cliffs, NJ.
This book is an excellent guide for parents or teachers and is intended to help them obtain services for handicapped children. The book contains exercises, forms, planning charts, and specific examples to help illustrate how school systems work. Although this book is not intended for preschoolers only and deals more with issues related to grade school, parents of preschoolers may find it a helpful preview of what is to come. The content of the book in a workshop format has been extensively field tested with parents.

Bateman, B. 1980. *So You're Going to a Hearing: Preparing for a Public Law 94–142 Due Process Hearing.* Research Press, Champaign, IL.
This booklet is intended for parents or advocates interested in preparing for a due process hearing. Sections are arranged chronologically, in the order of what usually happens before, during, and after the due process hearing. Some of the issues addressed include: program appropriateness, related services, private tutoring, evaluation, back tuition, suspension, and expulsion of a handicapped child.

Des Jardins, C. 1980. *How to Organize an Effective Parent/ Advocacy Group and Move Bureaucracies.* Coordinating Council for Handicapped Children, Chicago, IL. (Address: 407 S. Dearborn, Chicago, IL   60605.)
This is a step-by-step guide for parents of handicapped children, instructing them in how to get involved and how to be

assertive in obtaining services. Included are instructions for forming an advocacy group, how to lobby and get results, how to operate a program and get funding for it, and how to stay in control.

Lillie, D., and Place, P. 1982. *Partners: A Guide to Working with Schools, for Parents of Special Needs Children.* Scott, Foresman & Co., Glenview, IL.
This book provides important information to parents to prepare them to assume an active role in educational planning. Topics discussed include legal rights, definitions of handicapping conditions, and strategies for participating in your child's individualized education program (IEP) conference and in the evaluation process. A unique feature is the workbook format of the book. Practice activities are included that provide an opportunity for readers to assess their understanding of the material.

Martin, R. 1979. *Educating Handicapped Children: The Legal Mandate.* Research Press, Champaign, IL.
This paperback book is an excellent resource for information about Public Law 94–142, as it was originally conceived. Although there may be upcoming changes in the understanding or implementation of this law in the future, still relevant is the book's review of key concepts and regulations. The text is somewhat technical, because it uses terminology cited in the law, but it is still readable.

Parents Can be the Key to an Appropriate Education for Their Handicapped Child. 1981. PACER (Parent Advocacy Coalition for Educational Rights) Center, Inc., Pacer Center, 4701 Chicago Avenue South, Minneapolis, MN   55407.
This 28-page booklet includes information on parents' rights, parental involvement in assessment and IEP development, and appeals procedures. A helpful addition is a list of questions frequently asked by parents, as well as a list of advocacy agencies.

Parents Train Parents: A Plan and a Program. 1981. (Also published by PACER Center.)
This booklet gives a description of a model for reaching and informing parents of handicapped children about their rights and responsibilities under state and federal laws. PACER Center, Inc., is the operational base of Parents Train Parents, which was established in 1976 through a coalition of 18 organizations in Minnesota that shared concerns for handicapped children and their parents. This booklet is aimed toward potential adopters of the PACER program.

Turnbull, A.P., Strickland, B., and Brantley, J.C. 1982. *Developing and Implementing Individualized Education Programs.* 2nd Ed. Charles E. Merrill Publishing Co., Columbus, OH.
This book provides a detailed and comprehensive description of individualized education programs (IEPs). A chapter is included on each of the required components of IEPs (e.g., annual goals, objectives, and evaluation procedures) with practical suggestions for writing IEPs that are functional and explicit. Parents are likely also to be interested in chapters on related services and on participation in IEP meetings.

NATIONAL LEGAL RIGHTS AND ADVOCACY ORGANIZATIONS

Center for Law and Education (CLE), Gutman Library, 3rd Floor, 6 Appian Way, Cambridge, MA 02138. Robert Pressman, Dir., (617)495–4666.
Center on Human Policy (CHP), 216 Ostrom Ave., Syracuse, NY 13210. Steven Taylor, Assoc. Dir., (315)423–3851.
Children's Defense Fund (CDF), 1520 New Hampshire Avenue N.W., Washington, DC 20036. Marian Wright Edelman, Pres. (202)483–1470.
The Council for Exceptional Children (CEC), 1920 Association Drive, Reston, VA 22091. Richard L. McDowell, Pres., (703) 620–3660.

The National Center for Law and the Handicapped, Inc., 1235 North Eddy St., South Bend, IN 46617.

Mental Health Law Project (MHLP), 2021 L St., Suite 800, Washington, DC 20036. Norman S. Rosenberg, Dir., (202)467–5730.

Mexican American Legal Defense and Educational Fund (MALDEF), 28 Geary St., San Francisco, CA 94108. Vilma S. Martinez, Pres., (415)981–5800.

National Center for Youth Law (NCYL), 1663 Mission St., 5th Floor, San Francisco, CA 94103. John O'Toole, Dir., (415) 543–3307.

Native American Rights Fund (NARF), 1506 Broadway, Boulder, CO 80302. John E. Echohawk, Dir., (303)447–8760.

MEDIA AND CHILDREN'S BOOKS

Many parents are interested in obtaining books or materials about handicapped children to use with their other nonhandicapped children, neighborhood children, or to recommend to their child's teacher. Therefore, the following list contains children's stories about handicapped characters, bibliographies of children's books about handicaps, and types of media (films and tapes) developed for children that feature handicapped characters.

Bisshopp, P. 1978. *Books about Handicaps for Children and Young Adults: The Meeting Street School Annotated Bibliography.* The Meeting Street School, East Providence, RI.
This book contains annotated references to over 100 books for young children dealing with handicaps. Books are organized according to grade level and type of handicap (deafness and hearing impairment, blindness and visual impairment, orthopedic handicaps, mental retardation and brain damage, learning disabilities, speech problems, and emotional dysfunction). The annotations are thorough and substantive, and full bibliographic information is provided for easy access. In addition, the books have been evaluated by the author based on two criteria: 1) positive, realistic

portrayal of handicapped persons; and 2) quality of the work as literature. Books are noted as "recommended," or "not recommended," or no recommendation is included (which means they have both good and bad features).

Brightman, A.J. 1976. *Like Me.* Little, Brown & Co., Boston.
This is a thoroughly delightful story, written in simple rhyming text, about what the word "retarded" means. A young boy explains that being "like me" is also "like you" in many ways: "As you get to know us/You'll see what I mean/But you won't see the word/On our faces." The book contains many color photographs taken at a camp for retarded children, where Brightman worked for many years. Children as well as adults will find this book entertaining and educational.

Butler, D. 1980. *Cushla and Her Books.* 1st American Ed. Horn Books, Boston.
This book was written by the grandmother of Cushla, a physically and mentally handicapped child whose mother carefully documented her development from birth. Descriptions of, and excerpts from, Cushla's favorite stories, poems, and illustrations are given as well as the particular need that each book met for Cushla at a particular stage of development. The appendix contains lists of all the books in Cushla's library, the ages at which they were read, and a chart showing Cushla's reactions to the books, thus providing parents with an excellent source of children's literature.

Lass, B., and Bromfield, M. 1981. Books about children with special needs: An annotated bibiography. *The Reading Teaching,* 34(5): 530–533.
This is a much shorter annotated bibliography of children's books, but parents might want to make a photocopy of the list from the library if either of the above are not available.

Sullivan, M.B., and Bourke, L. 1980. *A Show of Hands.* Addison-Wesley Publishing Co., Inc., Reading, MA.
This is an educational book that is written especially for

children. It introduces them to the world of deaf people and to the use of sign language. The illustrations are humorous, artistic, and very effective.

FILMS/VIDEOTAPES

A Place in the Mainstream. Open Window Films, Berkeley, CA. Available through: Education Development Center, 55 Chapel St., Newton, MA   02160, (617)969–7100.This is a 16mm, 16-minute film. Rental: $20 for three days. Sale: $250 or $225 in video format.
This film is a document of the interactions of disabled and nondisabled three- , four- , and five-year-olds in a public school mainstreamed class. The types of children the viewer is introduced to include: Jason, a brain damaged child who interacts with a visitor in a wheelchair; normally rambunctious Proton, playing gently with Katherine who has delayed muscle development; Jamal, a visually impaired boy whose worries about the first day of school are eased by the fact that many of his classmates are wearing glasses; and Robin, an autistic child who leaves his special world for a while to interact with some of the other children.

Feeling Free. 1978. Scholastic Magazines, Inc. Available from: Scholastics' Feeling Free, 904 Sylvan Ave., Englewood Cliffs, NJ   07632.
This is a series of 16mm films, available for rental by writing to the distributor. Sale of films: $195 each. Video format: $136.50 each. Library of books and instructional kit: $99.50. The Feeling Free series includes six individual films, all depicting a child with a particular handicap interacting with a group of peers, who are also handicapped in some way. Each film presents an accurate picture of specific handicapping conditions (e.g., blindness, cerebral palsy, learning disability, and mental retardation) by having the handicapped children actually play themselves.

Kelly. Open Window Films, Berkeley, CA. Available through: Education Development Center, 55 Chapel St., Newton, MA   02160, (617)969–7200.

This is a 16mm, 27-minute color film. Rental: $25 for three days. Sale: $375.

This film documents the progress of Kelly Dixon, who was the first child with cerebral palsy to enter a regular child care program in the Berkeley, California, public schools. Kelly was three years old when she began her two years in the program. The film illustrates her progress and contains interviews with some of the key people involved in this mainstreaming effort. This would be a useful film to show to parents or to school personnel who are anxious about initiating a mainstreaming effort.

The Invisible Children. 1980. Learning Corporation of America, NY. Available from: Learning Corporation of America, 1350 Avenue of the Americas, New York, NY 10019, (212)397–9360. This is a 16mm, 24-minute film. Rental: $35. Sale: $350 for either 16mm or video format.

In "The Invisible Children" actor Gary Burghoff, himself a handicapped person, and the "Kids of the Block" puppets explain how handicapped children are both like and unlike children without disabilities. This film stresses the uniqueness of every person, and how the loss of things like sight or hearing represents a very small part of the total human being. The puppets, each one representing a different handicap, appear before a group of children and encourage them to ask questions. Renaldo, a "blind" puppet, leads a demonstration showing how to help guide a blind person. Mandy, who is deaf, demonstrates sign language. Mark, who has cerebral palsy, talks about how it affects his speech and what his life is like in a wheelchair. The emphasis is on how a handicapped child can lead a normal life. The use of puppets as guides in this film is an effective approach for lessening children's apprehension about asking questions, and accepting handicapped individuals on an equal basis. A teacher's guide is also available, which contains introductory material, discussion questions, teaching suggestions, a Braille and American Manual alphabet, a bibliography for children, a bibliography for teachers and parents, and a list of resource organizations and their addresses.

Young & Special. 1982. Crystal Kaiser, Ph.D. Available from:
University Park Press, 300 North Charles Street, Baltimore, MD
21201, (800)638–7511. This is a 30 videotape program available
in VHS, ¾-inch, and Beta II formats.
This is a videocassette program that trains and prepares
early childhood personnel faced with the tasks and problems of mainstreaming. It is a complete course that is a relevant, practical, and cost-effective model for both in-service
and preservice training. With normal early development as
an integral part of the program, *Young & Special* includes all
frequently occurring handicaps. It includes all levels of severity, and covers specialty topics such as child abuse and
working with the gifted, the chronically ill, and the termi-
nally ill. The program contains 30 learning modules, each
consisting of a 30-minute color videotape with case study
examples, a leader's guide for directing discussions and activities (includes all reading materials), terminology guides,
handouts, and bibliographies.

SPECIALIZED POPULATIONS

This section lists several references that deal specifically with a
particular type of handicap or disability, and contains suggestions for parents to read further about their own child's disability, if they desire.

American Physical Therapy Association. *Publications for Parents and Educators of Handicapped Children.* Available from:
The American Physical Therapy Association, 1156 15th St., Washington, DC   20005, (202)466–2070.
This publication contains a list of pamphlets, books, and per-
iodicals that are useful to parents of handicapped children.
Some of the topics included are: physical activities and recreation for individuals with handicapping conditions, rights
of the handicapped, and teaching and testing. The focus of
this bibliography is on physically handicapped children.

Atwell, A.A., and Clabby, D.A. 1975. *The Retarded Child: Answers to Questions Parents Ask.* Western Psychological Services, Los Angeles, CA.

This book provides basic facts and information on mental retardation. Written in question-and-answer format, it is easy to read. This could be a helpful resource to families who are involved in long-term planning for their child. Topics covered include sex education, institutionalization, vocational planning, and legal provisions.

Fisher, J. 1978. *A Parent's Guide to Learning Disabilities.* Charles Scribner's Sons, New York.
This book provides a lot of information in straightforward, nontechnical language in areas of interest to parents of learning disabled children, such as auditory processing, speech and language, hyperactivity, and minimal brain dysfunction. Each chapter includes excellent, brief case studies and ends with very specific recommendations for parents.

Jeffree, D.M., and McConkey, R. 1977. *Let Me Speak.* Taplinger Publishing Co., New York.
Based on research conducted by the authors, this book contains games and activities that parents can use with their children who are slow in acquiring language skills. Useful additions to the book are language development charts, which relate to many of the activities described.

Kauffman, J.M. 1977. *Characteristics of Children's Behavior Disorders.* Charles E. Merrill Publishing Co., Columbus, OH.
This book contains descriptions of the typical problems and characteristics of children with behavior disorders. It is not a "how-to" text, but it does cover some theory and research that may be illuminating to parents who wish to read further on this topic. (*Note:* Parents who primarily want to read about how to control the emotionally disturbed or behaviorally disordered child at home should refer to the specific resource section, "Parent Training," especially the books by Baker et al. and by Patterson.)

McArthur, S.H. 1982. *Raising Your Hearing-impaired Child: A Guide for Parents.* Alexander Graham Bell Association for the Deaf, Washington, DC.

This is a very basic book written by a former teacher, who has also raised two hearing-impaired daughters. The book includes topics that the author felt parents in particular should be informed about: basic information about a hearing loss; evaluating your own child; and suggested academic and communication skills that parents might need to reinforce when their hearing-impaired child is at the preschool, elementary school, and junior or senior high school levels. The book is not too heavily referenced, which has the advantage of being easy to read, but which runs the risk of being biased. For example, there is little reference to signing or to manual communication approaches. However, the author of this book is sensitive to living with a hearing-impaired child during the early years and how important it is to prepare the child for initial entry into kindergarten or elementary school.

Murphy, A.T. (ed.). 1979. The families of hearing-impaired children. *Volta Review,* 81(5).
This monograph contains a collection of articles by professionals in the area of hearing impairment, some of whom are also parents of hearing-impaired children. There are 13 articles, all fairly nontechnical and easy to read. The following three entries might be of particular interest to parents of hearing-impaired preschoolers: "Discovering and Accepting Hearing Impairment: Initial Reaction of Parents," "Parent-Infant Programs for Preschool Deaf Children: The Example of John Tracy Clinic," and "Members of the Family: Sisters and Brothers of Handicapped Children."

Orlansky, M.D., and Heward, W.L. 1981. *Voices: Interviews with Handicapped People.* Charles E. Merrill Publishing Co., Columbus, OH.
This book is a collection of short, insightful, and candid interviews with handicapped people, including young children and adults. The interviews are written in the first person, and offer the reader an understanding of how these handicapped people view their disability and the quality of their lives. An increased understanding of how to enhance positive adjustment of handicapped children is a major benefit of this book for parents.

Ulrich, S., and Wolf, A.W.M. 1972. *Elizabeth.* University of Michigan Press, Ann Arbor, MI.
The authors of this book describe the first five years in the life of a blind child. In addition to offering some practical and useful ideas for home training, the authors provide information on the education of the blind child.

Willoughly, D. 1979. *A Resource Guide for Parents and Educators of Blind Children.* National Federation of the Blind, Baltimore. Available from: National Federation of the Blind, 1800 Johnson St., Baltimore, MD   21230.
This resource is mainly for parents who want a thorough list of available pamphlets, agencies, and written material related to the special needs of blind children.

JOURNAL

The Exceptional Parent, Psy-Ed Corporation, 296 Boylston St., 3rd floor, Boston, MA   02116.
This bi-monthly publishes practical, informative articles written for parents. Here are some titles of recent articles to illustrate the diversity of material in each issue: Parent-School Disagreements, Baseball for Children with Disabilities, Models for Respite Care, Estate Planning, and Siblings of Children with Disabilities.

PARENT AND CONSUMER ORGANIZATIONS FOR HANDICAPPED CHILDREN

Many parents of preschool handicapped children may be interested in contacting one or more of these agencies to obtain printed materials and information on their services. Parents may also want to inquire about whether state and local chapters have been established. Although the presiding director of the agencies may change over time, the address and agency title are less likely to do so.

General

American Coalition of Citizens with Disabilities (ACCD), 1200 15th St., N.W., Suite 201, Washington, DC 20005. Frank Bowe, Dir., (202)785–4265.

March of Dimes Birth Defects Foundation (MDBDF), 1275 Mamaroneck Ave., White Plains, NY 10605. Charles L. Massey, Pres., (914)428–7100.

National Association for the Education of Young Children (NAEYC), 1834 Connecticut Ave., N.W., Washington, DC 20009. Marilyn Smith, Exec. Dir., (202)232–8777.

National Committee, Arts for the Handicapped (NCAH), 1701 K St., N.W., Suite 905, Washington, DC 20006. Bette Valenti, Exec. Officer, (202)332–6960.

National Therapeutic Recreation Society (NTRS), c/o National Recreation and Park Assn., 1601 N. Kent St., Arlington, VA 22209. Yvonne A. Washington, Staff Liaison, (703)525–0606.

Parents Campaign for Handicapped Children and Youth (PCHCY), Closer Look, Box 492, Washington, DC 20013. Barbara Scheiber, Exec. Dir.

Autism

The National Society for Children and Adults with Autism (NSAC-NSCAA), 1234 Massachusetts Ave., N.W., Suite 1017, Washington, DC 20005. Frank Warren, Exec. Dir., (202) 783–0215.

Blind

American Council of the Blind (ACB), 1211 Connecticut Ave., N.W., Suite 506, Washington, DC 20036. Oral O. Miller, Natl. Rep., (202)833–1251.

American Foundation for the Blind (AFB), 15 W. 16th St., New York, NY 10011. William F. Gallagher, Exec. Dir., (212) 620–2000.

American Printing House for the Blind (APH), P.O. Box 6085, 1839 Frankfort Ave., Louisville, KY 40206. Carson Y. Nolan, Pres., (502)895-2405.

National Association for the Visually Handicapped (NAVH), 305

East 24th St., New York, NY   10010. Lorraine Marchi, Exec. Dir., (212)889–3141.

National Federation of the Blind (NFB), 1800 Johnson St., Baltimore, MD   21230. Kenneth Jernigan, Pres., (301)659–9314.

Cerebral Palsy

American Academy for Cerebral Palsy and Developmental Medicine (AACPDM), P.O. Box 11083, Richmond, VA   23230. John A. Hinckley, Exec. Dir.

National Association of Sports for the Cerebral Palsied (NASCP), 66 E. 34th St., New York, NY   10016. Craig A. Huber, Dir.

National Easter Seal Society (NESS), 2023 W. Ogden Ave., Chicago, IL   60612. John Garrison, Exec. Dir., (312)243–8400.

United Cerebral Palsy Associations (UCPA), 66 E. 34th St , New York, NY   10016. Earl H. Cunerd, Exec. Dir., (212)481–6300.

Deaf and Hearing Impaired

Alexander Graham Bell Association for the Deaf (AGBAD), 3417 Volta Pl., N.W., Washington, DC   20007. Sara Conlon, Exec. Dir., (202)337–5220.

American Deafness and Rehabilitation Association (ADARA), 814 Thayer Ave., Silver Spring, MD   20910. Sharon H. Carter, Exec. Dir., (301)589–0880.

American Athletic Association for the Deaf (AAAD), 10604 E. 95th St. Terrace, Kansas City, MO   64134. Lyle Mortensen, Sec.-Treas.

International Association of Parents of the Deaf (IAPD), 814 Thayer Ave., Silver Spring, MD   20910. Jacqueline Z. Mendelsohn, Exec. Dir., (301)585–5400.

National Association of the Deaf (NAD), 814 Thayer Ave., Silver Spring, MD   20910. Albert T. Pimentel, Exec. Dir., (301) 587–1788.

Emotional Disturbance

American Association of Psychiatric Services for Children (AAPSC), 1725 K St., N.W., Washington, DC   20006. William E. Stone, Exec. Dir., (202)659–9115.

National Mental Health Association National Headquarters

(NMHA), 1800 North Kent St., Rosslyn, VA   22209. Robert B. Herman, Exec. Dir., (703)528–6405.

Epilepsy

Epilepsy Foundation of America (EFA), 4351 Garden City Dr., Landover, MD 29781. William McLin, Exec. Dir., (301)459–3700.

Learning Disabilities

Association for Children and Adults with Learning Disabilities (ACLD), 4156 Library Rd., Pittsburgh, PA   15234. Jean Peterson, Exec. Dir., (412)341–1515.

Mental Retardation

American Association of University Affliated Programs for the Developmentally Disabled (AAUAP), 1234 Massachusetts Ave., N.W., Washington, DC   20005. Seldon Tod, Exec. Dir., (202) 333–7880.

American Association on Mental Deficiency (AAMD), 5101 Wisconsin Ave., N.W., Washington, DC   20016. Albert J. Berkowitz, Exec. Dir., (202)686–5400.

Association for Retarded Citizens (ARC), 2501 Ave. J, Arlington, TX   76011. Philip Roos, Exec. Dir., (817)261–4961.

National Association for Down's Syndrome (NADS), Box 63, Oak Park, IL   60303. Sheila Hebein, Exec. Dir., (312)543–6060.

National Down's Syndrome Society (NDSS), 146 East 57th St., New York, NY 10022. Elizabeth F. Goodwin, Pres., (212)421–9800.

Special Olympics (SO), 1701 K St., N.W., Suite 203, Washington, DC   20006. Eunice Kennedy Shriver, Pres., (202)331–1346.

Physically Handicapped

American Occupational Therapy Association (AOTA), 1383 Piccard D., Suite 301, Rockville, MD   20850. James J. Garibaldi, Exec. Dir., (301)948–9626.

American Orthotic and Prosthetic Association (AOPA), 717 Pendleton St., Alexandria, VA   22314. William L. McCulloch, Exec. Dir.

American Physical Therapy Association (APTA), 1156 15th St., N.W., Washington, DC 20005. Royce P. Noland, CAE, Exec. Dir., (202)466–2070.

National Center for a Barrier Free Environment (NCBFE), 1140 Connecticut Ave., N.W., Washington, DC 20036. John W. Armstrong, Exec. Dir., (202)466–6896.

National Easter Seal Society (NESS), 2023 W. Ogden Ave., Chicago, IL 60612. John Garrison, Exec. Dir., (312)243–8400.

National Spinal Cord Injury Association (NSCIA), 269 Elliot St., Newton Upper Falls, MA 02164. Robert J. McHugh, Exec. Dir., (617)964–0521.

Spina Bifida Association of America (SBAA), 343 S. Dearborn Ave., Suite 319, Chicago, IL 60604. Kent Smith, Exec. Dir., (312)663–1562.

Severely Handicapped

The Association for the Severely Handicapped (TASH), 7010 Roosevelt Way, N.E., Seattle, WA 98115. Liz Lindley, Exec. Dir., (206)523–8446.

Speech Impaired

American Speech-Language-Hearing Association (ASHA), 10801 Rockville Pike, Rockville, MD 20852. Frederick T. Spahr, Exec. Dir., (301)897–5700.

Index

PARENT RESPONSE FORM

Dear Parent,

By the time you've finished reading this book we will already be trying to think of ways to revise it to make it more useful for parents. We would greatly appreciate it if you would take a few minutes to answer the following questions. You can write directly on this page and then cut out along the dotted line. Mail the completed Response Form to:

Dr. Jan Blacher
School of Education
University of California
Riverside, CA 92521

We look forward to hearing from you and, in advance, thank you for your cooperation.

(1) What sections of this book did you find <u>most</u> useful?

_____

_____

(2) What sections of this book did you find <u>least</u> useful?

_____

_____

(3) Did you read selected sections of this book, or did you read it from cover to cover? Please explain.

_____

_____

(4) Do you have any favorite books, articles, films, or organizations that you wish could be added to the resources section? If so, please give as complete a reference as you can:

_____

_____

(5) What suggestions do you have for improving the book to make it more useful to parents?

_____

_____

About the Authors

Pam Winton has been involved with parents of young handicapped children as a special education teacher, a parent support group leader, a researcher, and an advocate. She is also the parent of two young children.

Ann Turnbull has both personal and professional interests in parent issues. She has a teen-aged son who is mentally retarded. Professionally, she has conducted research and written extensively on how parents adapt to and grow with a handicapped child.

Jan Blacher is currently studying the effects of early education on young severely handicapped children and their families. She has coordinated an educational program that teaches parents how to handle a variety of child difficulties.